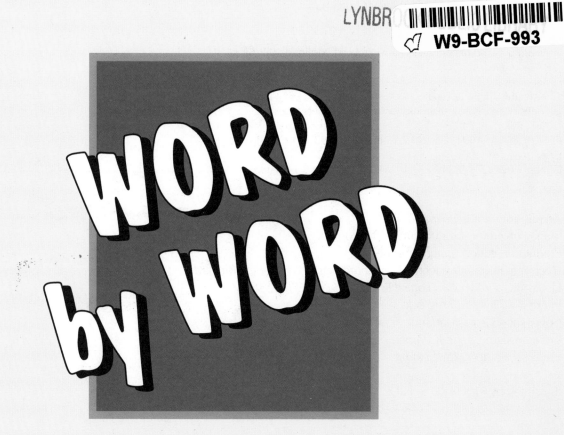

WORD by WORD

PICTURE DICTIONARY

Steven J. Molinsky · Bill Bliss

PRENTICE HALL REGENTS, Englewood Cliffs, New Jersey 07632

Library of Congress Cataloging-in-Publication Data

Molinsky, Steven J.
 Word by word picture dictionary / Steven J. Molinsky, Bill Bliss.
  p.   cm.
 Includes index.
 1. Picture dictionaries. English
2. English language – Textbooks for foreign speakers.
I. Bliss, Bill.   II. Title.
PE1629.M58   1994   423'.1 –dc20   93-21129 CIP
ISBN 0-13-278319-3
ISBN 0-13-278235-9 (pbk.)

Acquisitions editor: *Tina Carver*
Managing editor, production: *Sylvia Moore*
Production editor: *Janet Johnston*
Electronic production technology coordinator: *Molly Pike Riccardi*
Electronic production: *Louise B. Capuano*
Interior design: *Kenny Beck*
Cover supervisor: *Marianne Frasco*
Cover design: *Merle Krumper*
Buyer/scheduler: *Ray Keating*

Illustrated by RICHARD E. HILL

© 1994 by Prentice Hall Regents
Prentice-Hall, Inc.
A Simon & Schuster Company
Englewood Cliffs, New Jersey 07632

Printed in the United States of America

10   9   8   7   6

ISBN 0-13-278319-3 (case)
ISBN 0-13-278235-9 (paper)

Prentice-Hall International (UK) Limited, *London*
Prentice-Hall of Australia Pty. Limited, *Sydney*
Prentice-Hall Canada Inc., *Toronto*
Prentice-Hall Hispanoamericana, S. A., *Mexico*
Prentice-Hall of India Private Limited, *New Delhi*
Prentice-Hall of Japan, Inc., *Tokyo*
Simon & Schuster Asia Pte. Ltd., *Singapore*
Editora Prentice-Hall do Brasil, Ltda., *Rio de Janeiro*

The *Word by Word* Picture Dictionary presents more than 3,000 vocabulary words through lively full-color illustrations. This innovative Picture Dictionary offers students the essential vocabulary they need to communicate effectively in a wide range of relevant situations and contexts.

Word by Word organizes the vocabulary into 100 thematic units, providing a careful sequence of lessons that range from the immediate world of the student to the world at large. Early units on the family, the home, and daily activities lead to lessons on the community, school, workplace, shopping, recreation, and other topics. *Word by Word* offers extensive coverage of important lifeskill competencies and the vocabulary of school subjects and extracurricular activities. Since each unit is self-contained, *Word by Word* can be used either sequentially or in any desired order.

For users' convenience, the units in *Word by Word* are listed two ways: sequentially in the Table of Contents, and alphabetically in the Thematic Index. These resources, combined with the Glossary in the appendix, allow students and teachers to quickly and easily locate all words and topics in the Picture Dictionary.

The *Word by Word* Picture Dictionary is the centerpiece of the complete *Word by Word* Vocabulary Development Program, which offers a wide selection of print and media support materials for instruction at all levels. Ancillary materials include Workbooks at three different levels (Literacy, Beginning, and Intermediate), a Teacher's Resource Book, a Handbook of Vocabulary Teaching Strategies, a complete Audio Program, Wall Charts, Color Transparencies, Vocabulary Game Cards, a Song Album and accompanying Song Book, and a Testing Program. Bilingual editions of the Picture Dictionary are also available.

Teaching Strategies

Word by Word presents vocabulary words in context. Model conversations depict situations in which people use the words in meaningful communication. These models become the basis for students to engage in dynamic, interactive conversational practice. In addition, writing and discussion questions in each unit encourage students to relate the vocabulary and themes to their own lives as they share experiences, thoughts, opinions, and information about themselves, their cultures, and their countries. In this way, students get to know each other "word by word."

In using *Word by Word*, we encourage you to develop approaches and strategies that are compatible with your own teaching style and the needs and abilities of your students. You may find it helpful to incorporate some of the following techniques for presenting and practicing the vocabulary in each unit.

1. *Previewing the Vocabulary:* Activate students' prior knowledge of the vocabulary either by brainstorming with students the words in the unit they already know and writing them on the board, or by having students look at the Wall Chart, the transparency, or the illustration in *Word by Word* and identify the words they are familiar with.

2. *Presenting the Vocabulary:* Point to the picture of each word, say the word, and have the class repeat it chorally and individually. Check students' understanding and pronunciation of the vocabulary.

3. *Vocabulary Practice:* Have students practice the vocabulary as a class, in pairs, or in small groups. Say or write a word, and have students point to the item or tell the number. Or, point to an item or give the number, and have students say the word.

4. *Model Conversation Practice:* Some units have model conversations that use the first word in the vocabulary list. Other models are in the form of *skeletal dialogs*, in which vocabulary words can be inserted. (In many skeletal dialogs, bracketed numbers indicate which words can be used to practice the conversation. If no bracketed numbers appear, all the words on the page can be used.)

The following steps are recommended for Model Conversation Practice:

   a. Preview: Students look at the model illustration and discuss who they think the speakers are and where the conversation takes place.

   b. The teacher presents the model and checks students' understanding of the situation and the vocabulary.

   c. Students repeat each line of the conversation chorally or individually.

   d. Students practice the model in pairs.

   e. A pair of students presents a new conversation based on the model, but using a different word from the vocabulary list.

   f. In pairs, students practice several new conversations based on the model, using different vocabulary words.

   g. Pairs present their conversations to the class.

5. *Additional Conversation Practice:* Many units provide two additional skeletal dialogs for further conversation practice with the vocabulary. (These can be found in a yellow-shaded area at the bottom of the page.) Have students practice and present these conversations using any words they wish.

6. *Writing and Spelling Practice:* Have students practice spelling the words as a class, in pairs, or in small groups. Say or spell a word, and have students write it and then point to the picture of the item or tell the number. Or, point to a picture of an item or give the number, and have students write the word.

7. *Themes for Discussion, Composition, Journals, and Portfolios:* Each unit of *Word by Word* provides one or more questions for discussion and composition. (These can be found in a green-shaded area at the bottom of the page.) Have students respond to the questions as a class, in pairs, or in small groups. Or, have students write their responses at home, share their written work with other students, and discuss as a class, in pairs, or in small groups.

Students may enjoy keeping a journal of their written work. If time permits, you may want to write a response in each student's journal, sharing your own opinions and experiences as well as reacting to what the student has written. If you are keeping portfolios of students' work, these compositions serve as excellent examples of students' progress in learning English.

8. *Communication Activities:* The *Word by Word* Teacher's Resource Book provides a wealth of games, tasks, brainstorming, discussion, movement, drawing, miming, role-playing, and other activities designed to take advantage of students' different learning styles and particular abilities and strengths. For each unit, choose one or more of these activities to reinforce students' vocabulary learning in a way that is stimulating, creative, and enjoyable.

Word by Word aims to offer students a communicative, meaningful, and lively way of practicing English vocabulary. In conveying to you the substance of our program, we hope that we have also conveyed the spirit: that learning vocabulary can be genuinely interactive . . . relevant to our students' lives . . . responsive to students' differing strengths and learning styles . . . and fun!

Steven J. Molinsky
Bill Bliss

A. What's your **name**?
B. *Nancy Ann Peterson.*

1. name
2. first name
3. middle name
4. last name/family name/ surname
5. address
6. street number
7. street
8. apartment number
9. city
10. state
11. zip code
12. area code
13. telephone number/ phone number
14. social security number

A. What's your _____?
B. ....
A. Did you say ....?
B. Yes. That's right.

A. What's your last name?
B. ....
A. How do you spell that?
B. ....

Tell about yourself:
My name is ....
My address is ....
My telephone number is ....
Now interview a friend.

A. Who is she?
B. She's my **wife**.
A. What's her name?
B. Her name is *Betty*.

A. Who is he?
B. He's my **husband**.
A. What's his name?
B. His name is *Fred*.

1. wife
2. husband

parents
3. mother
4. father

children
5. daughter
6. son
7. sister
8. brother
9. baby

grandparents
10. grandmother
11. grandfather

grandchildren
12. granddaughter
13. grandson

A. I'd like to introduce my _____.
B. Nice to meet you.
C. Nice to meet you, too.

A. What's your _____'s name?
B. His/Her name is ....

Tell about your family.
Talk about photos of family members.

A. Who is she?
B. She's my **aunt**.
A. What's her name?
B. Her name is *Linda*.

A. Who is he?
B. He's my **uncle**.
A. What's his name?
B. His name is *Jack*.

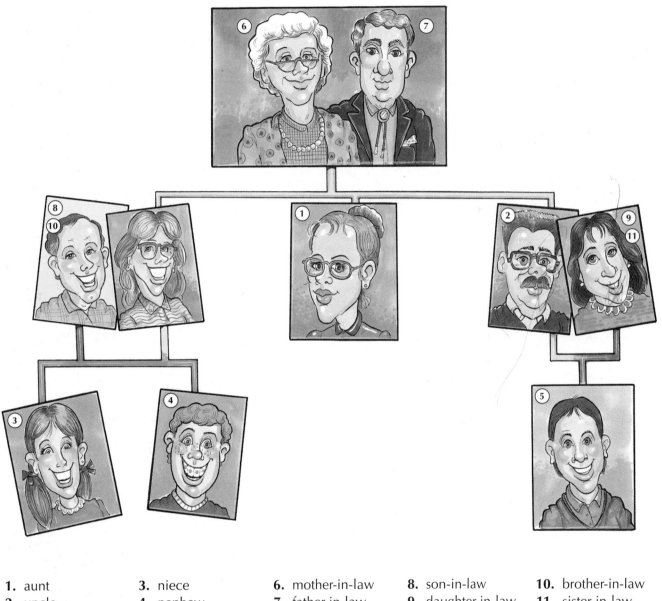

1. aunt
2. uncle
3. niece
4. nephew
5. cousin
6. mother-in-law
7. father-in-law
8. son-in-law
9. daughter-in-law
10. brother-in-law
11. sister-in-law

A. Is he/she your _____?
B. No. He's/She's my _____.
A. Oh. What's his/her name?
B. ....

A. Let me introduce my _____.
B. I'm glad to meet you.
C. Nice meeting you, too.

Tell about your relatives:
   What are their names?
   Where do they live?
Draw your family tree and talk
   about it.

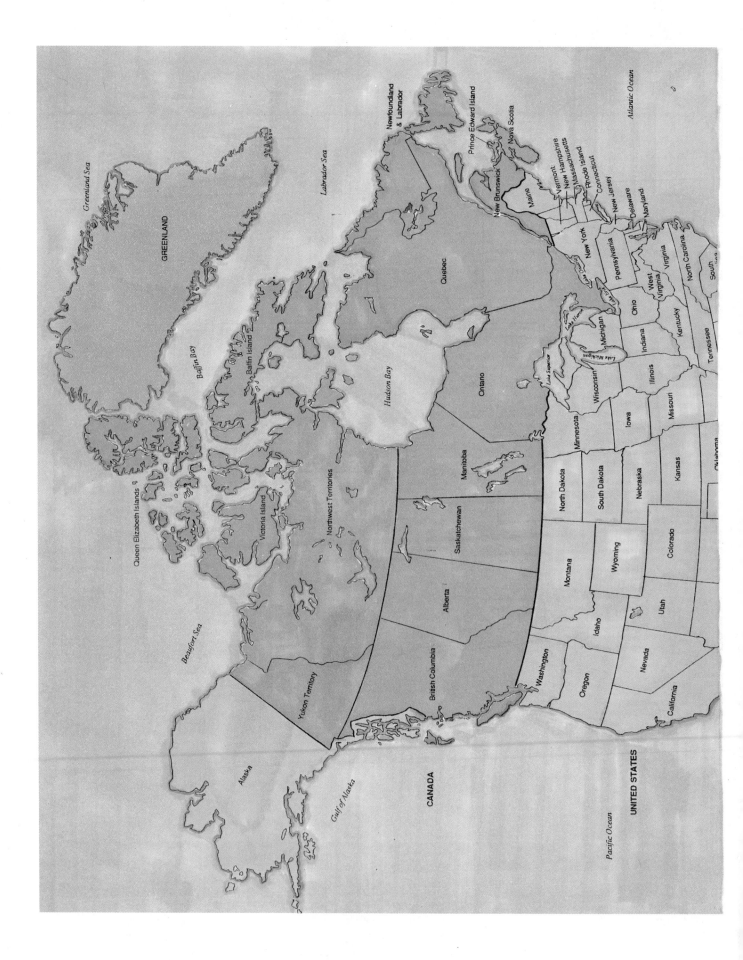

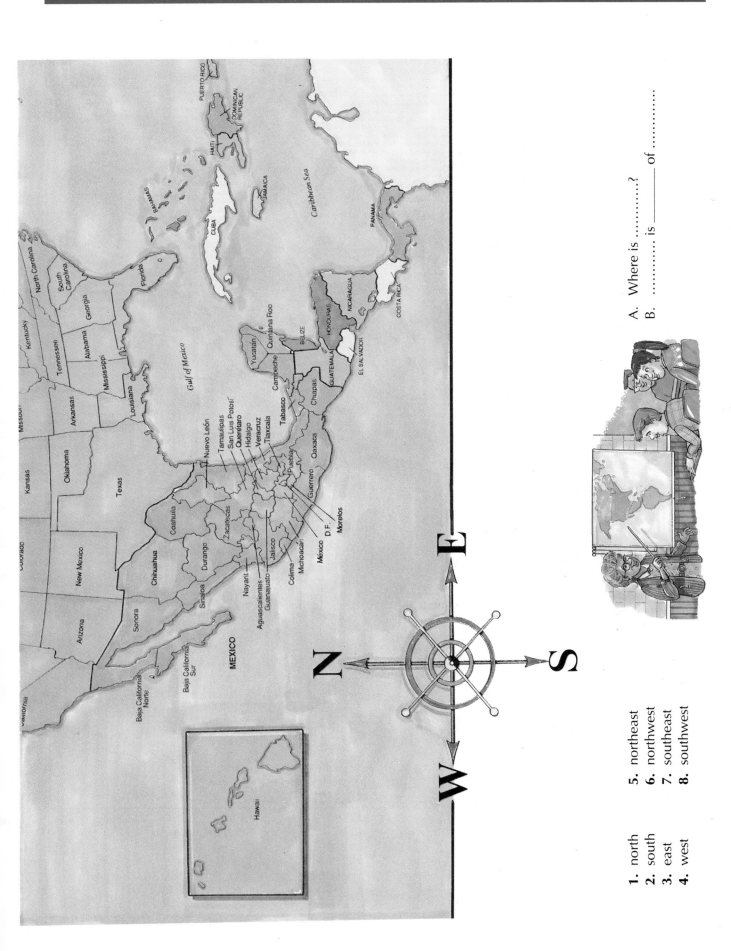

1. north
2. south
3. east
4. west

5. northeast
6. northwest
7. southeast
8. southwest

A. Where is ....?
B. .... is ——— of ....

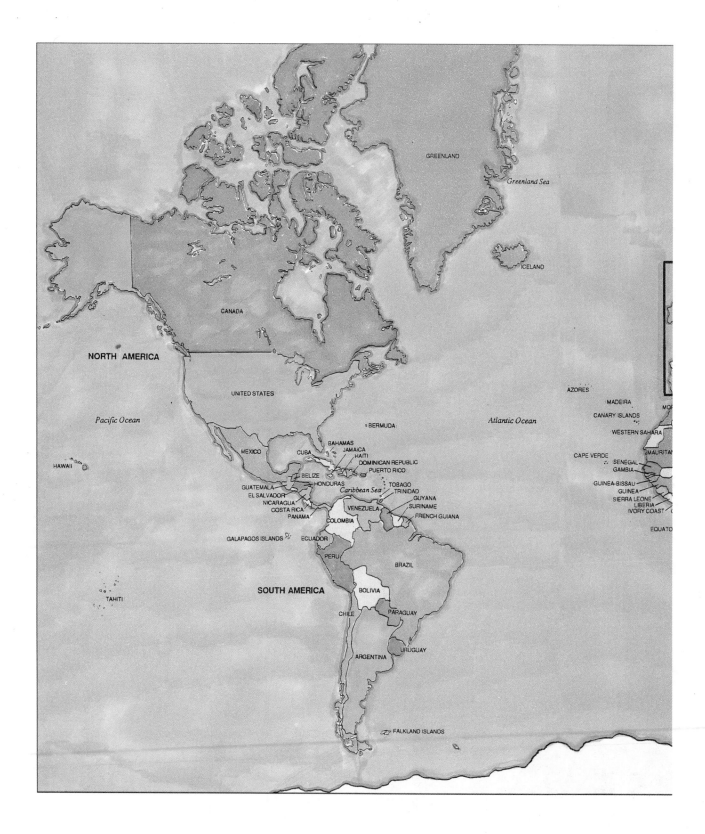

1. North America
2. South America
3. Europe
4. Africa
5. The Middle East
6. Asia
7. Australia
8. Antarctica

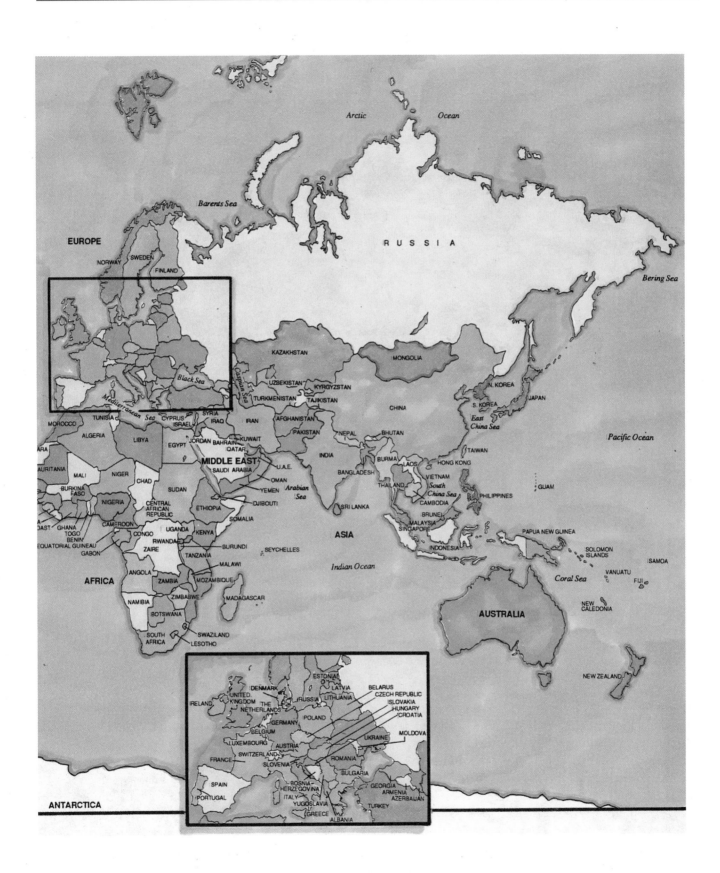

A. Where's ....?
A. What ocean/sea is near ....?
B. It's in _____.
B. The .... Ocean/Sea.

A. What do you do every day?
B. I **get up**, I **take a shower**, and I **brush my teeth**.

1. get up
2. take a shower
3. brush *my** teeth
4. floss *my** teeth
5. shave
6. get dressed

7. wash *my** face
8. put on makeup
9. brush *my** hair
10. comb *my** hair
11. make the bed

12. get undressed
13. take a bath
14. go to bed
15. sleep

16. make breakfast
17. make lunch
18. cook/make dinner
19. eat/have breakfast
20. eat/have lunch
21. eat/have dinner

* my, his, her, our, your, their

A. What does he do every day?
B. He _____s, he _____s, and he _____s.

A. What does she do every day?
B. She _____s, she _____s, and she _____s.

What do you do every day? Make a list.
Interview some friends and tell about their everyday activities.

A. Hi! What are you doing?
B. I'm **clean**ing **the apartment**.

1. clean the apartment/ clean the house
2. sweep the floor
3. dust
4. vacuum
5. wash the dishes

6. do the laundry
7. iron
8. feed the baby
9. feed the cat
10. walk the dog

11. watch TV
12. listen to the radio
13. listen to music
14. read
15. play

16. play basketball
17. play the guitar
18. practice the piano
19. study
20. exercise

A. Hi, ...! This is ....
    What are you doing?
B. I'm _____ing. How about you?
A. I'm _____ing.

A. Are you going to _____ today?
B. Yes. I'm going to _____ in a
    little while.

What are you going to do tomorrow?
Make a list of *everything* you are
going to do.

A. Where's the **teacher**?
B. The **teacher** is *next to* the **board**.

A. Where's the **pen**?
B. The **pen** is *on* the **desk**.

1. teacher
2. teacher's aide
3. student
4. seat/chair
5. pen
6. pencil
7. eraser
8. desk
9. teacher's desk

10. book/textbook
11. notebook
12. notebook paper
13. graph paper
14. ruler
15. calculator
16. clock
17. flag
18. board

19. chalk
20. chalk tray
21. eraser
22. P.A. system/
    loudspeaker
23. bulletin board
24. thumbtack
25. map
26. pencil sharpener

27. globe
28. bookshelf
29. overhead projector
30. TV
31. (movie) screen
32. slide projector
33. computer
34. (movie) projector

A. Is there a/an _____ in your
   classroom?*
B. Yes. There's a/an _____
   next to/on the _____.

*With 12, 13, 19 use: Is there _____ in your classroom?

A. Is there a/an _____ in your
   classroom?*
B. No, there isn't.

Describe your classroom.
(There's a/an ....)

Practice these classroom actions.

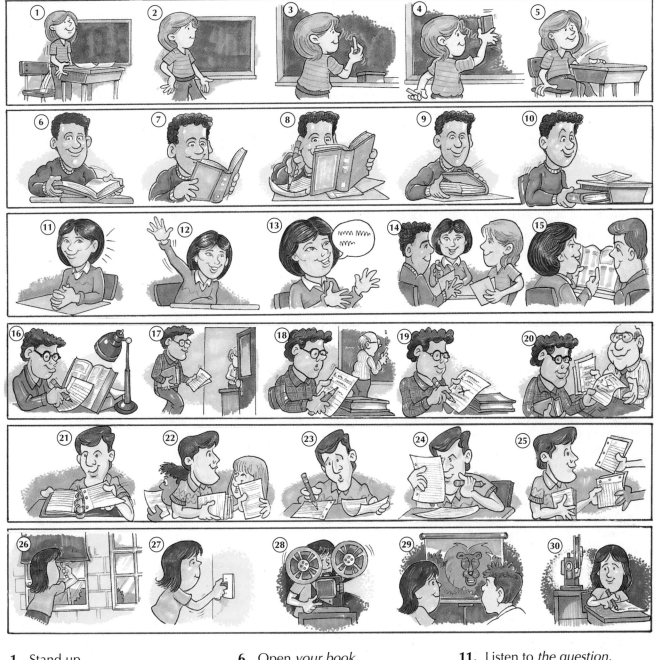

1. Stand up.
2. Go to the *board*.
3. Write *your name*.
4. Erase *your name*.
5. Sit down./Take *your seat*.

6. Open *your book*.
7. Read *page eight*.
8. Study *page eight*.
9. Close *your book*.
10. Put away *your book*.

11. Listen to *the question*.
12. Raise *your hand*.
13. Give *the answer*.
14. Work *in groups*.
15. Help *each other*.

16. Do *your homework*.
17. Bring in *your homework*.
18. Go over *the answers*.
19. Correct *your mistakes*.
20. Hand in *your homework*.

21. Take out *a piece of paper*.
22. Pass out *the tests*.
23. Answer *the questions*.
24. Check *your answers*.
25. Collect *the tests*.

26. Lower *the shades*.
27. Turn off *the lights*.
28. Turn on *the projector*.
29. Watch *the movie*.
30. Take notes.

You're the teacher!
Give instructions to your students.

A. Where are you from?
B. I'm from **Mexico**.

A. What's your nationality?
B. I'm **Mexican**.

A. What language do you speak?
B. I speak **Spanish**.

Country	Nationality	Language	Country	Nationality	Language
Afghanistan	Afghan	Afghan	Italy	Italian	Italian
Argentina	Argentine	Spanish	Japan	Japanese	Japanese
Australia	Australian	English	Jordan	Jordanian	Arabic
Bolivia	Bolivian	Spanish	Korea	Korean	Korean
Brazil	Brazilian	Portuguese	Laos	Laotian	Laotian
Cambodia	Cambodian	Cambodian	Latvia	Latvian	Latvian
Canada	Canadian	English/French	Lithuania	Lithuanian	Lithuanian
Chile	Chilean	Spanish	Malaysia	Malaysian	Malay
China	Chinese	Chinese	Mexico	Mexican	Spanish
Colombia	Colombian	Spanish	New Zealand	New Zealander	English
Costa Rica	Costa Rican	Spanish	Nicaragua	Nicaraguan	Spanish
Cuba	Cuban	Spanish	Panama	Panamanian	Spanish
(The) Dominican Republic	Dominican	Spanish	Peru	Peruvian	Spanish
Ecuador	Ecuadorian	Spanish	(The) Philippines	Filipino	Tagalog
Egypt	Egyptian	Arabic	Poland	Polish	Polish
El Salvador	Salvadorean	Spanish	Portugal	Portuguese	Portuguese
England	English	English	Puerto Rico	Puerto Rican	Spanish
Estonia	Estonian	Estonian	Romania	Romanian	Romanian
Ethiopia	Ethiopian	Amharic	Russia	Russian	Russian
France	French	French	Saudi Arabia	Saudi	Arabic
Germany	German	German	Spain	Spanish	Spanish
Greece	Greek	Greek	Taiwan	Taiwanese	Chinese
Guatemala	Guatemalan	Spanish	Thailand	Thai	Thai
Haiti	Haitian	Haitian Kreyol	Turkey	Turkish	Turkish
Honduras	Honduran	Spanish	Ukraine	Ukrainian	Ukrainian
Indonesia	Indonesian	Indonesian	(The) United States	American	English
Israel	Israeli	Hebrew	Venezuela	Venezuelan	Spanish
			Vietnam	Vietnamese	Vietnamese

A. What's your native language?
B. _____.
A. Oh. What country are you from?
B. _____.

A. Where are you and your husband/wife going on your vacation?
B. We're going to _____.
A. That's nice. Tell me, do you speak _____?
B. No, but my husband/wife does. He's/She's _____.

Tell about yourself:
    Where are you from?
    What's your nationality?
    What languages do you speak?
Now interview and tell about a friend.

A. Where do you live?
B. I live in an **apartment building**.

  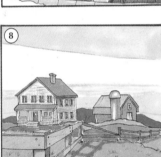 

1. apartment (building)
2. (single-family) house
3. duplex/two-family house
4. townhouse/townhome

5. condominium/condo
6. dormitory/dorm
7. mobile home/trailer
8. farmhouse

9. cabin
10. nursing home
11. shelter
12. houseboat

A. Town Taxi Company.
B. Hello. Please send a taxi to
   (address) .
A. Is that a house or an apartment?
B. It's a/an _____.
A. All right. We'll be there right
   away.

A. This is the Emergency Operator.
B. Please send an ambulance to
   (address) .
A. Is that a private home?
B. It's a/an _____.
A. What's your name?
B. ....
A. And your telephone number?
B. ....

Tell about people you know and the
types of housing they live in.
Discuss:
  Who lives in dormitories?
  Who lives in nursing homes?
  Who lives in shelters?
  Why?

A. Where are you?
B. I'm in the living room.
A. What are you doing?
B. I'm *dusting** the **coffee table**.

*dusting/cleaning

1. coffee table
2. rug
3. floor
4. armchair
5. end table
6. lamp
7. lampshade
8. window

9. drapes/curtains
10. sofa/couch
11. (throw) pillow
12. ceiling
13. wall
14. wall unit/ entertainment unit

15. television
16. video cassette recorder/VCR
17. stereo system
18. speaker
19. loveseat
20. plant

21. painting
22. frame
23. mantel
24. fireplace
25. fireplace screen
26. picture/photograph
27. bookcase

A. You have a lovely living room!
B. Oh, thank you.
A. Your _____ is/are beautiful!
B. Thank you for saying so.

A. Uh-oh! I just spilled coffee on your _____!
B. That's okay. Don't worry about it.

Tell about your living room.
(In my living room there's ....)

A. This **dining room table** is very nice.
B. Thank you. It was a gift from my *grandmother.**

*grandmother/grandfather/aunt/uncle/...

1. (dining room) table	**7.** salad bowl	**13.** candle	**19.** teapot
2. (dining room) chair	**8.** pitcher	**14.** centerpiece	**20.** coffee pot
3. china cabinet	**9.** serving bowl	**15.** salt shaker	**21.** creamer
4. china	**10.** serving platter	**16.** pepper shaker	**22.** sugar bowl
5. chandelier	**11.** tablecloth	**17.** butter dish	
6. buffet	**12.** candlestick	**18.** serving cart	

[In a store]

A. May I help you?
B. Yes, please. Do you have
  _____s?*
A. Yes. _____s* are right over there.
B. Thank you.

*With 4, use the singular.

[At home]

A. Look at this old _____
  I just bought!
B. Where did you buy it?
A. At a yard sale. How do you
  like it?
B. It's VERY unusual!

Tell about your dining room.
(In my dining room there's ....)

A. Excuse me. Where does the **salad plate** go?
B. It goes *to the left of* the **dinner plate**.

A. Excuse me. Where does the **soup spoon** go?
B. It goes *to the right of* the **teaspoon**.

A. Excuse me. Where does the **wine glass** go?
B. It goes *between* the **water glass** and the **cup and saucer**.

A. Excuse me. Where does the **cup** go?
B. It goes *on* the **saucer**.

1. salad plate
2. bread-and-butter plate
3. dinner plate
4. soup bowl

5. water glass
6. wine glass
7. cup
8. saucer
9. napkin

silverware
10. salad fork
11. dinner fork
12. knife

13. teaspoon
14. soup spoon
15. butter knife

A. Waiter? Excuse me. This _____ is dirty.
B. I'm terribly sorry. I'll get you another _____ right away.

A. Oops! I dropped my _____!
B. That's okay! I'll get you another _____ from the kitchen.

Practice giving directions. Tell someone how to set a table. (Put the ....)

A. Ooh! Look at that big bug!!
B. Where?
A. It's on the **bed**!
B. I'LL get it.

1. bed	**10.** bedspread	**18.** mirror	**27.** bunk bed
2. headboard	**11.** comforter/quilt	**19.** jewelry box	**28.** trundle bed
3. pillow	**12.** footboard	**20.** dresser/bureau	**29.** sofa bed/
4. pillowcase	**13.** blinds	**21.** twin bed	convertible sofa
5. fitted sheet	**14.** night table/	**22.** mattress	**30.** day bed
6. (flat) sheet	nightstand	**23.** box spring	**31.** cot
7. blanket	**15.** alarm clock	**24.** double bed	**32.** water bed
8. electric blanket	**16.** clock radio	**25.** queen-size bed	**33.** canopy bed
9. dust ruffle	**17.** chest (of drawers)	**26.** king-size bed	**34.** hospital bed

[In a store]

A. Excuse me. I'm looking for
 a/an _____.*
B. We have some very nice _____s.
 And they're all on sale this week.
A. Oh, good!

*With 13, use: Excuse me. I'm looking for _____.

[In a bedroom]

A. Oh, no! I just lost my
 contact lens!
B. Where?
A. I think it's on the _____.
B. I'll help you look.

Tell about your bedroom.
(In my bedroom there's ....)

A. I think we need a new **dishwasher**.
B. I think you're right.

1. dishwasher	**10.** dish rack	**19.** stove/range	**28.** freezer
2. dishwasher detergent	**11.** paper towel holder	**20.** burner	**29.** ice maker
3. dishwashing liquid	**12.** dish towel	**21.** oven	**30.** ice tray
4. faucet	**13.** trash compactor	**22.** potholder	**31.** refrigerator magnet
5. (kitchen) sink	**14.** cabinet	**23.** toaster	**32.** kitchen table
6. (garbage) disposal	**15.** microwave (oven)	**24.** spice rack	**33.** placemat
7. sponge	**16.** (kitchen) counter	**25.** (electric) can opener	**34.** kitchen chair
8. scouring pad	**17.** cutting board	**26.** cookbook	**35.** garbage pail
9. pot scrubber	**18.** canister	**27.** refrigerator	

[In a store]

A. Excuse me. Are your _____s still on sale?
B. Yes, they are. They're twenty percent off.

[In a kitchen]

A. When did you get this/these new _____(s)?
B. I got it/them last week.

Tell about your kitchen.
(In my kitchen there's ....)

A. Could I possibly borrow your **wok**?
B. Sure. I'll get it for you right now.
A. Thanks.

1. wok	**12.** cake pan	**23.** (electric) mixer	**34.** cookie cutter
2. pot	**13.** pie plate	**24.** food processor	**35.** strainer
3. saucepan	**14.** cookie sheet	**25.** electric frying pan	**36.** garlic press
4. lid/cover/top	**15.** (mixing) bowl	**26.** waffle iron	**37.** bottle opener
5. frying pan/skillet	**16.** rolling pin	**27.** (electric) griddle	**38.** can opener
6. roasting pan	**17.** measuring cup	**28.** popcorn maker	**39.** whisk
7. roaster	**18.** measuring spoon	**29.** blender	**40.** (vegetable) peeler
8. double boiler	**19.** coffeemaker	**30.** grater	**41.** knife
9. pressure cooker	**20.** coffee grinder	**31.** (egg) beater	**42.** spatula
10. colander	**21.** tea kettle	**32.** ladle	**43.** paring knife
11. casserole (dish)	**22.** toaster oven	**33.** ice cream scoop	

A. What are you looking for?
B. I'm looking for the _____.*
A. Did you look in the drawers/
   in the cabinets/next to the
   _____/...........?
B. Yes. I looked everywhere!

*With 2, 4, 12–15, 41, use:
 I'm looking for a _____.

[A Commercial]

Come to *Kitchen World*! We have
everything you need for your kitchen,
from _____s and _____s, to
_____s and _____s. Are you
looking for a new _____? Is it time
to throw out your old _____? Come
to *Kitchen World* today! We have
everything you need!

What things do you have in your
   kitchen?
Which things do you use very often?
Which things do you rarely use?

A. Thank you for the **teddy bear.** It's a very nice gift.
B. You're welcome. Tell me, when are you due?
A. In a few more weeks.

1. teddy bear
2. intercom
3. chest (of drawers)
4. crib
5. crib bumper
6. mobile
7. crib toy
8. night light

9. changing table/ dressing table
10. stretch suit
11. changing pad
12. diaper pail
13. toy chest
14. doll
15. swing

16. playpen
17. stuffed animal
18. rattle
19. cradle
20. walker
21. car seat
22. stroller
23. baby carriage

24. food warmer
25. booster seat
26. baby seat
27. high chair
28. portable crib
29. baby carrier
30. potty

A. That's a very nice _____.
   Where did you get it?
B. It was a gift from ....

A. Do you have everything you need before the baby comes?
B. Almost everything. We're still looking for a/an _____ and a/an _____.

Tell about your country:
   What things do people buy for a new baby?
   Does a new baby sleep in a separate room, as in the United States?

[1–12]
A. Do we need anything from the store?
B. Yes. Could you get some more **baby powder**?
A. Sure.

[13–17]
A. Do we need anything from the store?
B. Yes. Could you get another **pacifier**?
A. Sure.

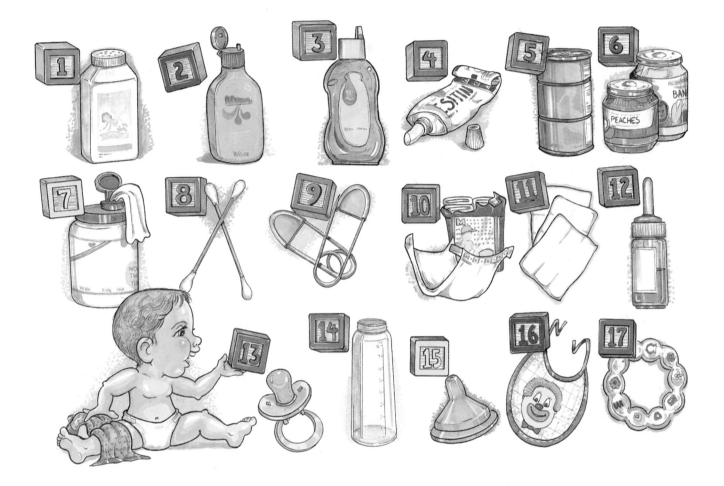

1. baby powder
2. baby lotion
3. baby shampoo
4. ointment
5. formula

6. baby food
7. (baby) wipes
8. cotton swabs
9. diaper pins

10. disposable diapers
11. cloth diapers
12. (liquid) vitamins
13. pacifier

14. bottle
15. nipple
16. bib
17. teething ring

[In a store]
A. Excuse me. I can't find the _____.*
B. I'm sorry. We're out of _____.* We'll have some more tomorrow.

[At home]
A. Honey? Where did you put the _____?
B. It's/They're in/on/next to the _____.

In your opinion, which are better: cloth diapers or disposable diapers? Why?
Tell about baby products in your country.

*With 13–17, use the plural.

A. Where's the **plunger**?
B. It's *next to* the **toilet**.

A. Where's the **toothbrush**?
B. It's *in* the **toothbrush holder**.

A. Where's the **washcloth**?
B. It's *on* the **towel rack**.

A. Where's the **mirror**?
B. It's *over* the **sink**.

1. plunger	**12.** washcloth/	**21.** hot water faucet	**32.** shower
2. toilet	facecloth	**22.** cold water faucet	**33.** shower curtain rod
3. toilet tank	**13.** hamper	**23.** cup	**34.** shower head
4. toilet seat	**14.** (bathroom) scale	**24.** toothbrush	**35.** shower curtain rings
5. air freshener	**15.** shelf	**25.** toothbrush holder	**36.** shower curtain
6. toilet paper holder	**16.** hair dryer	**26.** soap	**37.** bathtub/tub
7. toilet paper	**17.** fan	**27.** soap dish	**38.** drain
8. toilet brush	**18.** mirror	**28.** soap dispenser	**39.** rubber mat
9. towel rack	**19.** medicine cabinet/	**29.** Water Pik	**40.** sponge
10. bath towel	medicine chest	**30.** vanity	**41.** bath mat/bath rug
11. hand towel	**20.** (bathroom) sink	**31.** wastebasket	

A. [Knock. Knock.] Did I leave my glasses in there?
B. Yes. They're on/in/next to the _____.

A. *Bobby?*
B. Yes, Mom/Dad?
A. You didn't clean up the bathroom! There's toothpaste on the _____ and there's powder all over the _____!
B. Sorry, Mom/Dad. I'll clean it up right away.

Tell about your bathroom.
(In my bathroom there's ....)

[1–17]
A. Excuse me. Where can I find **toothbrush**es?
B. They're in the next aisle.
A. Thank you.

[18–38]
A. Excuse me. Where can I find **shampoo**?
B. It's in the next aisle.
A. Thank you.

1. toothbrush	**11.** nail clipper	**21.** toothpaste	**31.** nail polish
2. comb	**12.** nail brush	**22.** mouthwash	**32.** nail polish remover
3. (hair) brush	**13.** scissors	**23.** dental floss	
4. razor	**14.** tweezers	**24.** shaving creme	**makeup**
5. razor blades	**15.** bobby pins	**25.** after shave lotion	**33.** base/foundation
6. electric razor/ electric shaver	**16.** hair clips	**26.** deodorant	**34.** blush/rouge
7. styptic pencil	**17.** barrettes	**27.** powder	**35.** lipstick
8. shower cap	**18.** shampoo	**28.** hand lotion	**36.** eye shadow
9. nail file	**19.** conditioner/rinse	**29.** perfume/cologne	**37.** eye liner
10. emery board	**20.** hairspray	**30.** shoe polish	**38.** mascara

A. I'm going to the drug store to get a/an _____.*
B. While you're there, could you also get a/an _____?*
A. Sure.

*With 5, 13–38, use: get _____.

A. Do you have everything for the trip?
B. I think so.
A. Did you remember to pack your _____?
B. Oops! I forgot. Thanks for reminding me.

You're going on a trip. Make a list of personal care products you need to take with you.

[1–17, 28–39]
A. Excuse me. Do you sell **broom**s?
B. Yes. They're at the back of the store.
A. Thanks.

[18–27]
A. Excuse me. Do you sell **laundry detergent**?
B. Yes. It's at the back of the store.
A. Thanks.

1. broom
2. dustpan
3. whisk broom
4. feather duster
5. dust cloth
6. iron
7. ironing board
8. carpet sweeper
9. vacuum (cleaner)
10. vacuum cleaner attachments

11. vacuum cleaner bag
12. hand vacuum
13. (dust) mop/ (dry) mop
14. (sponge) mop
15. (wet) mop
16. washing machine/ washer
17. dryer

18. laundry detergent
19. fabric softener
20. bleach
21. starch
22. static cling remover
23. cleanser
24. window cleaner
25. ammonia
26. furniture polish
27. floor wax

28. paper towels
29. hanger
30. laundry basket
31. laundry bag
32. utility sink
33. scrub brush
34. sponge
35. bucket/pail
36. trash can/garbage can
37. recycling bin
38. clothesline
39. clothespins

A. How do you like this/these _____?
B. It's/They're great!

A. They're having a big sale at Dave's Discount Store this week.
B. Oh, really? What's on sale?
A. _[18–27]_ and _[1–17, 28–39]_ s.

Who does the cleaning and laundry in your home? What things does that person use?

A. When are you going to repair the **lamppost**?
B. I'm going to repair it next Saturday.

1. lamppost	**10.** window	**19.** gutter	**26.** satellite dish
2. mailbox	**11.** (window) screen	**20.** drainpipe/downspout	**27.** patio
3. front walk	**12.** shutter	**21.** deck	**28.** lawnmower
4. front steps	**13.** roof	**22.** back door	**29.** barbecue/
5. (front) porch	**14.** TV antenna	**23.** doorknob	(outdoor) grill
6. storm door	**15.** chimney	**24.** screen door	**30.** lawn chair
7. front door	**16.** garage	**25.** side door	**31.** tool shed
8. doorbell	**17.** garage door		
9. (front) light	**18.** driveway		

[On the telephone]
A. Harry's Home Repairs.
B. Hello. Do you fix _____s?
A. No, we don't.
B. Oh, okay. Thank you.

[At work on Monday morning]
A. What did you do this weekend?
B. Nothing much. I repaired my
_____ and my _____.

Do you like to repair things?
What things can you repair yourself?
What things can't you repair? Who
repairs them?

A. Is there a **lobby**?
B. Yes, there is. Do you want to see the apartment?
A. Yes, I do.

1. lobby
2. intercom
3. buzzer
4. mailbox
5. elevator
6. doorman

7. smoke detector
8. peephole
9. (door) chain
10. dead-bolt lock
11. air conditioner

12. fire alarm
13. garbage chute
14. laundry room
15. superintendent
16. storage room

17. parking garage
18. parking lot
19. balcony/terrace
20. swimming pool
21. whirlpool

[Renting an apartment]
A. Let me show you around the building.*
B. Okay.
A. This is the _____ and here's the _____.
B. I see.

*With 7–11, use:
  Let me show you around the apartment.

[On the telephone]
A. Mom and Dad? I found an apartment.
B. Good. Tell us about it.
A. It has a/an _____ and a/an _____.
B. That's nice. Does it have a/an _____?
A. Yes, it does.

Tell about the differences between living in a house and in an apartment building.

A. Did you remember to pay the **carpenter**?
B. Yes. I wrote a check yesterday.

1. carpenter
2. handyman
3. (house) painter
4. chimney sweep
5. appliance repair person

6. TV repair person
7. locksmith
8. gardener
9. electrician
10. plumber
11. exterminator

12. gas bill
13. electric bill
14. telephone bill
15. water bill
16. oil bill/heating bill

17. cable TV bill
18. pest control bill
19. rent
20. parking fee
21. mortgage payment

[1–11]
A. When is the _____ going to come?
B. This afternoon.

[12–21]
A. When is the _____ due?
B. It's due at the end of the month.

Tell about utilities, services, and repairs you pay for. How much do you pay?

A. Could I borrow your **hammer***?
B. Sure.
A. Thanks.

**With 28–32, use:* Could I borrow some _____s?

1. hammer	**9.** saw	**17.** power saw	**25.** paint thinner
2. screwdriver	**10.** hand drill	**18.** level	**26.** sandpaper
3. Phillips screwdriver	**11.** brace	**19.** plane	**27.** wire
4. wrench	**12.** chisel	**20.** toolbox	**28.** nail
5. pliers	**13.** scraper	**21.** (paint) pan	**29.** screw
6. hacksaw	**14.** vise	**22.** (paint) roller	**30.** washer
7. hatchet	**15.** electric drill	**23.** paintbrush/brush	**31.** bolt
8. monkey wrench	**16.** (drill) bit	**24.** paint	**32.** nut

[1–4, 6–27]
A. Where's the _____?
B. It's on/next to/near/over/under the _____.

[5, 28–32]
A. Where are the _____(s)?
B. They're on/next to/near/over/under the _____.

Do you like to work with tools?
What tools do you have in your home?

[1–16]
A. I can't find the **lawnmower**!
B. Look in the tool shed.
A. I did.
B. Oh! Wait a minute! I lent the **lawnmower** to the neighbors.

[17–32]
A. I can't find the **flashlight**!
B. Look in the utility cabinet.
A. I did.
B. Oh! Wait a minute! I lent the **flashlight** to the neighbors.

1. lawnmower
2. gas can
3. sprinkler
4. (garden) hose
5. nozzle
6. wheelbarrow
7. watering can
8. rake

9. hoe
10. trowel
11. shovel
12. hedge clippers
13. work gloves
14. vegetable seeds
15. fertilizer
16. grass seed

17. flashlight
18. fly swatter
19. extension cord
20. tape measure
21. step ladder
22. plunger
23. yardstick
24. mousetrap

25. batteries
26. lightbulbs/bulbs
27. fuses
28. electrical tape
29. oil
30. glue
31. bug spray/insect spray
32. roach killer

[1–11, 17–24]
A. I'm going to the hardware store. Can you think of anything we need?
B. Yes. We need a/an _____.
A. Oh, that's right.

[12–16, 25–32]
A. I'm going to the hardware store. Can you think of anything we need?
B. Yes. We need _____.
A. Oh, that's right.

What gardening tools and home supplies do you have? Tell about how and when you use each one.

Cardinal Numbers

1	one	11	eleven	21	twenty-one	101	one hundred (and) one
2	two	12	twelve	22	twenty-two	102	one hundred (and) two
3	three	13	thirteen	30	thirty	1,000	one thousand
4	four	14	fourteen	40	forty	10,000	ten thousand
5	five	15	fifteen	50	fifty	100,000	one hundred thousand
6	six	16	sixteen	60	sixty	1,000,000	one million
7	seven	17	seventeen	70	seventy		
8	eight	18	eighteen	80	eighty		
9	nine	19	nineteen	90	ninety		
10	ten	20	twenty	100	one hundred		

A. How old are you?
B. I'm _____ years old.

A. How many people are there in your family?
B. _____.

Ordinal Numbers

1st	first	11th	eleventh	21st	twenty-first	101st	one hundred (and) first
2nd	second	12th	twelfth	22nd	twenty-second	102nd	one hundred (and) second
3rd	third	13th	thirteenth	30th	thirtieth	1000th	one thousandth
4th	fourth	14th	fourteenth	40th	fortieth	10,000th	ten thousandth
5th	fifth	15th	fifteenth	50th	fiftieth	100,000th	one hundred thousandth
6th	sixth	16th	sixteenth	60th	sixtieth	1,000,000th	one millionth
7th	seventh	17th	seventeenth	70th	seventieth		
8th	eighth	18th	eighteenth	80th	eightieth		
9th	ninth	19th	nineteenth	90th	ninetieth		
10th	tenth	20th	twentieth	100th	one hundredth		

A. What floor do you live on?
B. I live on the _____ floor.

A. Is this the first time you've seen this movie?
B. No. It's the _____ time.

Arithmetic

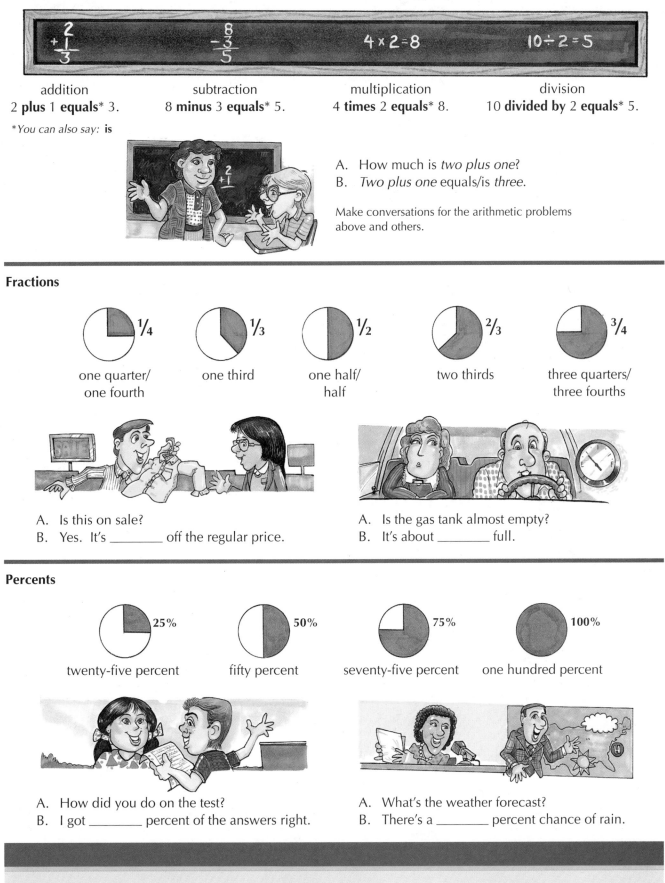

$$\begin{array}{c} 2 \\ +1 \\ \hline 3 \end{array} \qquad \begin{array}{c} 8 \\ -3 \\ \hline 5 \end{array} \qquad 4 \times 2 = 8 \qquad 10 \div 2 = 5$$

addition	subtraction	multiplication	division
2 **plus** 1 **equals*** 3.	8 **minus** 3 **equals*** 5.	4 **times** 2 **equals*** 8.	10 **divided by** 2 **equals*** 5.

You can also say: **is**

A. How much is *two plus one*?
B. *Two plus one* equals/is *three*.

Make conversations for the arithmetic problems above and others.

Fractions

¼	⅓	½	⅔	¾
one quarter/ one fourth	one third	one half/ half	two thirds	three quarters/ three fourths

A. Is this on sale?
B. Yes. It's _____ off the regular price.

A. Is the gas tank almost empty?
B. It's about _____ full.

Percents

25%	50%	75%	100%
twenty-five percent	fifty percent	seventy-five percent	one hundred percent

A. How did you do on the test?
B. I got _____ percent of the answers right.

A. What's the weather forecast?
B. There's a _____ percent chance of rain.

Research and discuss:
What percentage of the people in your country live in cities?
live on farms? work in factories? vote in national elections?

2:00
two o'clock

2:15
two fifteen/
a quarter after *two*

2:30
two thirty/
half past *two*

2:45
two forty-five
a quarter to *three*

2:05
two oh five

2:20
two twenty/
twenty after *two*

2:40
two forty/
twenty to *three*

2:55
two fifty-five
five to *three*

A. What time is it?
B. It's _____.

A. What time does the movie begin?
B. At _____.

two a.m.

two p.m.

noon/
twelve noon

midnight/
twelve midnight

A. When does the train leave?
B. At _____.

A. What time will we arrive?
B. At _____.

Tell about your daily schedule:
What do you do? When?
(I get up at _____. I ....)
Do you usually have enough time to do things, or do you run out of time? Explain.
If there were 25 hours in a day, what would you do with the extra hour? Why?

Tell about the use of time in different cultures or countries you are familiar with:
Do people arrive on time for work? appointments? parties?
Do trains and buses operate exactly on schedule?
Do movies and sports events begin on time?
Do workplaces use time clocks or timesheets to record employees' work hours?

1999 JANUARY 1999

SUN	MON	TUE	WED	THUR	FRI	SAT
					1	2
3	4	5	6	7	8	9
10	11	12	13	14	15	16
17	18	19	20	21	22	23
24/31	25	26	27	28	29	30

1. **year**

   nineteen ninety-nine

2. **month**

January	July
February	August
March	September
April	October
May	November
June	December

3. **day**

Sunday	Thursday
Monday	Friday
Tuesday	Saturday
Wednesday	

4. **date**

   January 2, 1999
   1/2/99
   January second, nineteen ninety-nine

A. What year is it?
B. It's _____.

A. What month is it?
B. It's _____.

A. What day is it?
B. It's _____.

A. What's today's date?
B. Today is _____.

When did you begin to study English?
What days of the week do you study English? (I study
   English on _____.)

When is your birthday? (My birthday is on _____.)
What are your favorite months of the year? Why?
What are your least favorite months of the year? Why?

A. Where are you going?
B. I'm going to the **appliance store**.

1. appliance store
2. auto dealer/car dealer
3. bakery
4. bank
5. barber shop
6. book store
7. bus station
8. cafeteria
9. child-care center/day-care center
10. cleaners/dry cleaners
11. donut shop
12. clinic
13. clothing store
14. coffee shop
15. computer store

16. concert hall
17. convenience store
18. copy center
19. delicatessen/deli
20. department store

21. discount store
22. drug store/pharmacy
23. flower shop/florist
24. furniture store
25. gas station/service station

26. grocery store
27. hair salon
28. hardware store
29. health club/spa
30. hospital

A. Hi! How are you today?
B. Fine. Where are you going?
A. To the _____. How about you?
B. I'm going to the _____.

A. Oh, no! I can't find my wallet/purse!
B. Did you leave it at the _____?
A. Maybe I did.

Which of these places are in your neighborhood?
(In my neighborhood there's a/an ....)

A. Where's the **hotel**?
B. It's right over there.

1. hotel	**6.** maternity shop	**11.** night club
2. ice cream shop	**7.** motel	**12.** park
3. jewelry store	**8.** movie theater	**13.** (parking) garage
4. laundromat	**9.** museum	**14.** parking lot
5. library	**10.** music store	**15.** pet shop

16. photo shop
17. pizza shop
18. post office
19. restaurant
20. school

21. shoe store
22. (shopping) mall
23. supermarket
24. theater
25. toy store

26. train station
27. travel agency
28. video store
29. vision center/eyeglass store
30. zoo

A. Is there a/an _____ nearby?
B. Yes. There's a/an _____ around the corner.

A. Excuse me. Where's the _____?
B. It's down the street, next to the _____.
A. Thank you.

Which of these places are in your neighborhood?
(In my neighborhood there's a/an ....)

A. Where's the _____?
B. On/In/Next to/Between/Across from/
In front of/Behind/Under/Over the _____.

1. trash container	**6.** street light	**11.** manhole	**16.** bus driver
2. police station	**7.** ice cream truck	**12.** bus stop	**17.** parking meter
3. jail	**8.** sidewalk	**13.** taxi/cab/taxicab	**18.** meter maid
4. courthouse	**9.** curb	**14.** taxi driver/cab driver	**19.** subway
5. bench	**10.** street	**15.** bus	**20.** subway station

21. utility pole
22. taxi stand
23. phone booth
24. public telephone
25. sewer

26. street sign
27. fire station
28. office building
29. drive-through window
30. fire alarm box

31. intersection
32. police officer
33. crosswalk
34. pedestrian

35. traffic light/traffic signal
36. garbage truck
37. newsstand
38. street vendor

[An Election Speech]
If I am elected mayor, I'll take care of all the problems we have in our city. We need to do something about our _____s. We also need to do something about our _____s. And look at our _____s! We REALLY need to do something about THEM! We need a new mayor who can solve these problems. If I am elected mayor, we'll be proud of our _____s, _____s, and _____s again! Vote for me!

Step outside. Look around.
Describe everything you see.

1–2	tall – short	27–28	new – old
3–4	long – short	29–30	young – old
5–6	large/big – small/little	31–32	good – bad
7–8	high – low	33–34	hot – cold
9–10	heavy/fat – thin/skinny	35–36	soft – hard
11–12	heavy – light	37–38	easy – difficult/hard
13–14	loose – tight	39–40	smooth – rough
15–16	fast – slow	41–42	neat – messy
17–18	straight – crooked	43–44	clean – dirty
19–20	straight – curly	45–46	noisy/loud – quiet
21–22	wide – narrow	47–48	married – single
23–24	thick – thin	49–50	rich/wealthy – poor
25–26	dark – light		

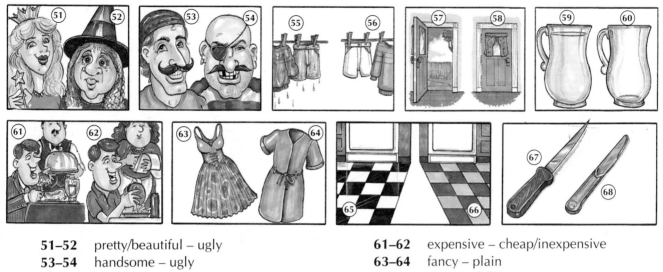

51–52	pretty/beautiful – ugly
53–54	handsome – ugly
55–56	wet – dry
57–58	open – closed
59–60	full – empty

61–62	expensive – cheap/inexpensive
63–64	fancy – plain
65–66	shiny – dull
67–68	sharp – dull

[1–2]
A. Is your sister **tall**?
B. No. She's **short**.

1–2	Is your sister _____?
3–4	Is his hair _____?
5–6	Is their dog _____?
7–8	Is the bridge _____?
9–10	Is your friend _____?
11–12	Is the box _____?
13–14	Are the pants _____?
15–16	Is the train _____?
17–18	Is the path _____?
19–20	Is his hair _____?
21–22	Is that street _____?
23–24	Is the line _____?
25–26	Is the room _____?
27–28	Is your car _____?
29–30	Is he _____?
31–32	Are your neighbor's children _____?
33–34	Is the water _____?

35–36	Is your pillow _____?
37–38	Is today's homework _____?
39–40	Is your skin _____?
41–42	Is your desk _____?
43–44	Are the dishes _____?
45–46	Is your neighbor _____?
47–48	Is your sister _____?
49–50	Is your uncle _____?
51–52	Is the witch _____?
53–54	Is the pirate _____?
55–56	Are the clothes _____?
57–58	Is the door _____?
59–60	Is the pitcher _____?
61–62	Is that restaurant _____
63–64	Is the dress _____?
65–66	Is your kitchen flo_
67–68	Is the knife ____

1. tired
2. sleepy
3. exhauste
4. hot

A. Tell me about your ....
B. He's/She's/It's/They're _____.

A. Is your .... _____?
B. No, not at all. As a matter of fact, he's/she's/it's/they're _____.

A. You look **tired**.
B. I am. I'm VERY **tired**.

	5. cold	9. sick/ill	13. miserable
	6. hungry	10. happy	14. pleased
ed	7. thirsty	11. ecstatic	15. disappointed
	8. full	12. sad/unhappy	16. upset

17. annoyed
18. frustrated
19. angry/mad
20. furious

21. disgusted
22. surprised
23. shocked
24. nervous

25. worried
26. scared/afraid
27. bored
28. proud

29. embarrassed
30. ashamed
31. jealous
32. confused

A. Are you _____?
B. No. Why do you ask? Do I LOOK _____?
A. Yes. You do.

A. I'm _____.
B. Why?
A. ....

What makes you happy? sad? mad?
When do you feel nervous? annoyed?
Do you ever feel embarrassed? When?

[1–22]
A. This **apple** is delicious!
   Where did you get it?
B. At *Shaw's Supermarket.*

[23–31]
A. These **grapes** are delicious!
   Where did you get them?
B. At *Farmer Fred's Fruit Stand.*

1. apple	**7.** nectarine	**13.** avocado	**18.** grapefruit	**25.** prunes
2. peach	**8.** kiwi	**14.** cantaloupe	**19.** lemon	**26.** dates
3. pear	**9.** papaya	**15.** honeydew	**20.** lime	**27.** raisins
4. banana	**10.** mango	(melon)	**21.** orange	**28.** blueberries
5. plum	**11.** fig	**16.** pineapple	**22.** tangerine	**29.** cranberries
6. apricot	**12.** coconut	**17.** watermelon	**23.** grapes	**30.** raspberries
			24. cherries	**31.** strawberries

A. I'm hungry. Do we have any fruit?
B. Yes. We have _____s* and
   _____s.*

A. Do we have any more _____s?†
B. No. I'll get some more when I go
   to the supermarket.

*With 14–18, use:
  We have _____ and _____.

†With 14–18, use:
  Do we have any more _____?

What are your most favorite fruits?
What are your least favorite fruits?
Which of these fruits grow where you
  live?
Name and describe other fruits you
  are familiar with.

A. What do we need from the supermarket?
B. We need **lettuce*** and **pea**s.†

*1–12   †13–36

1. lettuce	**13.** pea	**25.** potato
2. cabbage	**14.** string bean/green bean	**26.** sweet potato
3. celery	**15.** lima bean	**27.** yam
4. corn	**16.** black bean	**28.** green pepper
5. cauliflower	**17.** kidney bean	**29.** red pepper
6. broccoli	**18.** brussels sprout	**30.** beet
7. spinach	**19.** cucumber	**31.** onion
8. asparagus	**20.** tomato	**32.** scallion/green onion
9. eggplant	**21.** carrot	**33.** red onion
10. zucchini (squash)	**22.** radish	**34.** pearl onion
11. acorn squash	**23.** mushroom	**35.** turnip
12. butternut squash	**24.** artichoke	**36.** parsnip

A. How do you like the
   [1–12] / [13–36] s?
B. It's/They're delicious.

A. *Johnny?* Finish your vegetables!
B. But you KNOW I hate
   [1–12] / [13–36] s!
A. I know. But it's/they're good
   for you!

Which vegetables do you like?
Which vegetables don't you like?
Which of these vegetables grow where
   you live?
Name and describe other vegetables
   you are familiar with.

A. I'm going to the supermarket to get **milk** and **soup**.*
   Do we need anything else?
B. Yes. We also need **cereal** and **soda**.*

*With 43, 44, 46, 49, and 55, use: a _____.

A. Dairy Products
1. milk
2. low-fat milk
3. skim milk
4. chocolate milk
5. buttermilk
6. orange juice†
7. cheese
8. butter
9. margarine
10. sour cream
11. cream cheese

12. cottage cheese
13. yogurt
14. eggs

B. Canned Goods
15. soup
16. tuna fish
17. (canned) vegetables
18. (canned) fruit

C. Packaged Goods
19. cereal
20. cookies
21. crackers
22. spaghetti
23. noodles
24. macaroni
25. rice

D. Juice
26. apple juice
27. pineapple juice

28. grapefruit juice
29. tomato juice
30. fruit punch
31. grape juice
32. cranberry juice
33. juice paks
34. powdered drink mix

E. Beverages
35. soda
36. diet soda
37. bottled water

† Orange juice is not a dairy product, but is usually found in this section.

F. Poultry
38. chicken
39. chicken legs
40. drumsticks
41. chicken breasts
42. chicken wings
43. turkey
44. duck

G. Meat
45. ground beef
46. roast
47. steak
48. stewing meat

49. leg of lamb
50. lamb chops
51. pork
52. pork chops
53. ribs
54. sausages
55. ham
56. bacon

H. Seafood
FISH
57. salmon
58. halibut
59. flounder
60. swordfish
61. haddock
62. trout

SHELLFISH
63. oysters
64. scallops
65. shrimp
66. mussels
67. clams
68. crabs
69. lobster

I. Baked Goods
70. English muffins
71. cake
72. pita bread
73. rolls
74. bread

J. Frozen Foods
75. ice cream
76. frozen vegetables
77. frozen dinners
78. frozen lemonade
79. frozen orange juice

A. Excuse me. Where can I find [1–79] ?
B. In the [A–J] Section, next to the [1–79] .
A. Thank you.

A. Pardon me. I'm looking for [1–79] .
B. It's/They're in the [A–J] Section, between the [1–79] and the [1–79] .
A. Thanks.

Which of these foods do you like?
Which foods are good for you?
What brands of these foods do you buy?

[1–70]
A. Look! _____ is/are on sale this week!
B. Let's get some!

A. Deli
1. roast beef
2. bologna
3. salami
4. ham
5. turkey
6. corned beef
7. American cheese
8. Swiss cheese
9. provolone
10. mozzarella
11. cheddar cheese
12. potato salad
13. cole slaw
14. macaroni salad
15. seafood salad

B. Snack Foods
16. potato chips
17. corn chips
18. tortilla chips
19. nacho chips
20. pretzels
21. popcorn
22. nuts
23. peanuts

C. Condiments
24. ketchup
25. mustard
26. relish
27. pickles
28. olives
29. salt
30. pepper
31. spices
32. soy sauce
33. mayonnaise
34. (cooking) oil
35. olive oil
36. vinegar
37. salad dressing

D. Coffee and Tea
38. coffee
39. decaffeinated coffee/
    decaf coffee
40. tea
41. herbal tea
42. cocoa/
    hot chocolate mix

E. Baking Products
43. flour
44. sugar
45. cake mix

F. Jams and Jellies
46. jam
47. jelly
48. marmalade
49. peanut butter

G. Paper Products
50. tissues
51. napkins
52. toilet paper
53. paper cups
54. paper plates
55. straws
56. paper towels

H. Household Items
57. sandwich bags
58. trash bags
59. soap
60. liquid soap
61. aluminum foil
62. plastic wrap
63. waxed paper

I. Baby Products
64. baby cereal
65. formula
66. baby food
67. wipes
68. (disposable) diapers

J. Pet Food
69. cat food
70. dog food

K. Checkout Area
71. aisle
72. shopping cart
73. shopper/customer
74. checkout counter
75. conveyor belt
76. coupons
77. scanner

78. scale
79. cash register
80. cashier
81. plastic bag
82. paper bag
83. bagger/packer
84. express checkout (line)
85. tabloid (newspaper)
86. magazine
87. (chewing) gum
88. candy
89. shopping basket

A. Do we need __[1–70]__ ?
B. No, but we need __[1–70]__ .

A. We forgot to get __[1–70]__ !
B. I'll get it/them.
   Where is it?/Where are they?
A. In the __[A–J]__ Section over
   there.

Make a complete shopping list of
everything you need from the
supermarket.
Describe the differences between U.S.
supermarkets and food stores in
your country.

A. Would you please get a **bag** of *flour*
   when you go to the supermarket?
B. A **bag** of *flour?* Sure. I'd be happy to.

A. Would you please get two **head**s of *lettuce*
   when you go to the supermarket?
B. Two **head**s of *lettuce?* Sure. I'd be happy to.

1. bag	**4.** box	**7.** carton	**10.** ear
2. bar	**5.** bunch	**8.** container	**11.** head
3. bottle	**6.** can	**9.** dozen*	**12.** jar

* "a dozen eggs," NOT "a dozen of eggs."

13. loaf–loaves
14. pack
15. package
16. roll

17. six-pack
18. stick
19. tub

20. pint
21. quart
22. half-gallon

23. gallon
24. liter
25. pound

[At home]
A. What did you get at the supermarket?
B. I got _____, _____, and _____.

[In a supermarket]
A. Is this checkout counter open?
B. Yes, but this is the express line. Do you have more than eight items?
B. No. I only have _____, _____, and _____.

Open your kitchen cabinets and refrigerator. Make a list of all the things you find.
What do you do with empty bottles, jars, and cans? Do you recycle them, reuse them, or throw them away?

teaspoon
tsp.

tablespoon
Tbsp.

1 (fluid) ounce
1 fl. oz.

cup
8 fl. ozs.

pint
pt.
16 fl. ozs.

quart
qt.
32 fl. ozs.

gallon
gal.
128 fl. ozs.

A. How much water should I put in?
B. The recipe says to add one _____ of water.

A. This fruit punch is delicious! What's in it?
B. Two _____s of orange juice, three _____s of grape juice, and a _____ of apple juice.

an ounce

oz.

a quarter
of a pound
¼ lb.
4 ozs.

half a pound

½ lb.
8 ozs.

three-quarters
of a pound
¾ lb.
12 ozs.

a pound

lb.
16 ozs.

A. How much roast beef would you like?
B. I'd like _____, please.

A. This chili tastes very good! What did you put in it?
B. _____ of ground beef, _____ of beans, _____ of tomatoes, and _____ of chili powder.

A. Can I help?
B. Yes. Please **cut up** the *vegetables.*

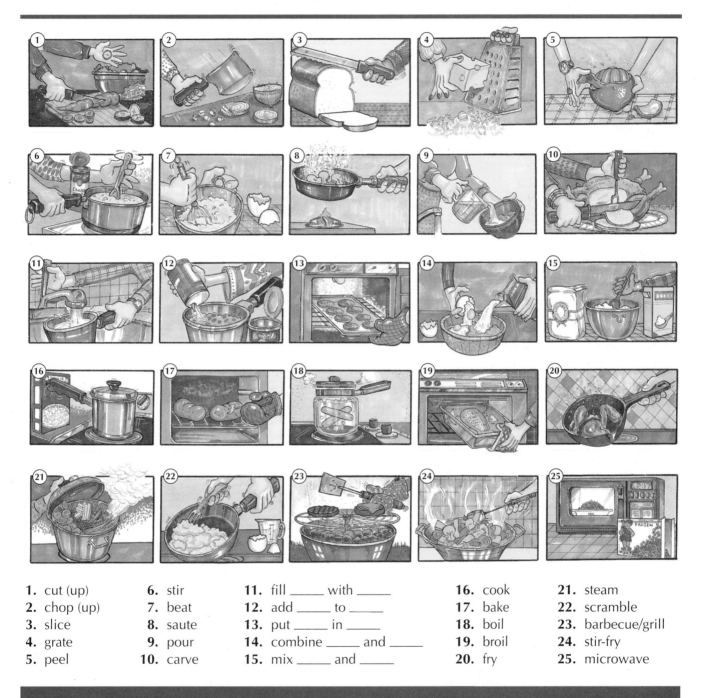

1. cut (up)	6. stir	11. fill _____ with _____	16. cook	21. steam
2. chop (up)	7. beat	12. add _____ to _____	17. bake	22. scramble
3. slice	8. saute	13. put _____ in _____	18. boil	23. barbecue/grill
4. grate	9. pour	14. combine _____ and _____	19. broil	24. stir-fry
5. peel	10. carve	15. mix _____ and _____	20. fry	25. microwave

[1–25]
A. What are you doing?
B. I'm _____ing the ....

[16–25]
A. How long should I _____ the ....?
B. For .... minutes/seconds.

What's your favorite recipe? Give instructions and use the
units of measure on page 52. For example:
  Mix a cup of flour and two tablespoons of sugar.
  Add half a pound of butter.
  Bake at 350° (degrees) for twenty minutes.

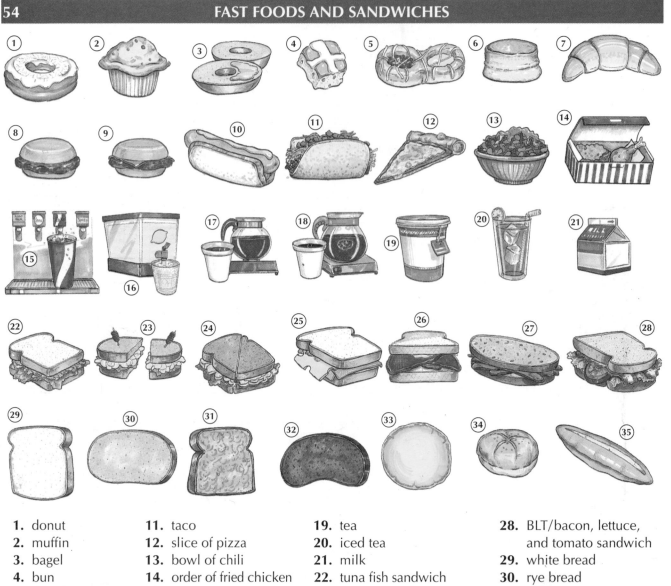

1. donut
2. muffin
3. bagel
4. bun
5. danish/pastry
6. biscuit
7. croissant
8. hamburger
9. cheeseburger
10. hot dog

11. taco
12. slice of pizza
13. bowl of chili
14. order of fried chicken
15. Coke/Diet Coke/ Pepsi/7–Up/...
16. lemonade
17. coffee
18. decaf coffee

19. tea
20. iced tea
21. milk
22. tuna fish sandwich
23. egg salad sandwich
24. chicken salad sandwich
25. ham and cheese sandwich
26. roast beef sandwich
27. corned beef sandwich

28. BLT/bacon, lettuce, and tomato sandwich
29. white bread
30. rye bread
31. whole wheat bread
32. pumpernickel
33. pita bread
34. a roll
35. a submarine roll

A. May I help you?
B. Yes. I'd like a/an [1–14] , please.
A. Anything to drink?
B. Yes. I'll have a small/medium-size/ large/extra-large [15–21] .

A. I'd like a [22–28] on [29–35] , please.
B. What do you want on it?
A. Lettuce/tomato/mayonnaise/mustard/...

Do you go to fast food restaurants or sandwich shops?
When? How often? What do you order?

A. Appetizers
1. fruit cup/fruit cocktail
2. tomato juice
3. shrimp cocktail
4. chicken wings
5. nachos
6. potato skins

B. Salads
7. tossed salad/ garden salad
8. Greek salad
9. spinach salad
10. antipasto (plate)
11. Caesar salad
12. salad bar

C. Main Courses/Entrees
13. meatloaf
14. roast beef/prime rib
15. veal cutlet
16. baked chicken
17. broiled fish
18. spaghetti and meatballs

D. Side Dishes
19. a baked potato
20. mashed potatoes
21. french fries
22. rice
23. noodles
24. mixed vegetables

E. Desserts
25. chocolate cake
26. apple pie
27. ice cream
28. jello
29. pudding
30. ice cream sundae

[Ordering dinner]

A. May I take your order?

B. Yes, please. For the appetizer I'd like the [1–6] .

A. And what kind of salad would you like?

B. I'll have the [7–12] .

A. And for the main course?

B. I'd like the [13–18] , please.

A. What side dish would you like with that?

B. Hmm. I think I'll have [19–24] .

[Ordering dessert]

A. Would you care for some dessert?

B. Yes. I'll have [25–29] /an [30] .

Do you go to restaurants? Which ones? What do you order?
Describe some popular desserts in your country.

A. What's your favorite color?
B. **Red.**

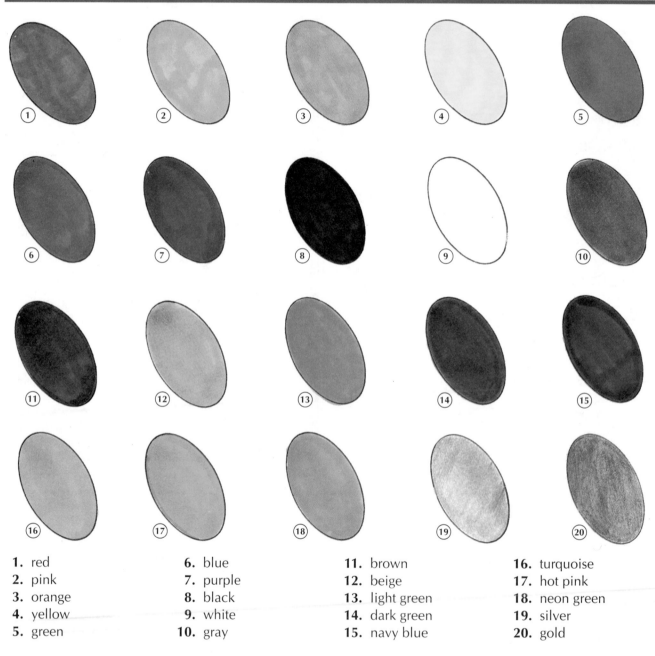

1. red	6. blue	11. brown	16. turquoise
2. pink	7. purple	12. beige	17. hot pink
3. orange	8. black	13. light green	18. neon green
4. yellow	9. white	14. dark green	19. silver
5. green	10. gray	15. navy blue	20. gold

A. I like your _____ shirt.
   You look very good in _____.
B. Thank you. _____ is my favorite
   color.

A. My color TV is broken.
B. What's the matter with it?
A. People's faces are _____,
   the sky is _____, and the
   grass is _____!

Do you know the flags of different
   countries? What are the colors of
   the flags you know?
What color makes you happy? What
   color makes you sad? Why?

A. I think I'll wear my new **shirt** today.
B. Good idea!

1. shirt/
   long-sleeved shirt
2. short-sleeved shirt
3. dress shirt
4. sport shirt
5. polo shirt/jersey/
   sport shirt
6. flannel shirt

7. blouse
8. turtleneck
9. pants/slacks
10. (blue) jeans
11. corduroy pants/
    corduroys
12. skirt
13. dress
14. jumpsuit

15. shorts
16. sweater
17. V-neck sweater
18. cardigan sweater
19. overalls
20. uniform
21. jacket/sports jacket/
    sports coat

22. jacket
23. blazer
24. suit
25. three-piece suit
26. vest
27. tie/necktie
28. bowtie
29. tuxedo
30. (evening) gown

A. I really like your _____.
B. Thank you.
A. Where did you get it/them?
B. At ....

A. Oh, no! I just ripped my _____!
B. What a shame!

What color clothes do you like to
   wear?
Do you ever wear jeans? When?
What do you wear at parties? at work
   or at school? at weddings?

1. pajamas
2. nightgown
3. nightshirt
4. bathrobe/robe
5. slippers
6. undershirt/ tee shirt
7. (jockey) shorts/ underpants
8. boxer shorts

9. athletic supporter/ jockstrap
10. long underwear/ long johns
11. (bikini) panties/ underpants
12. briefs
13. bra
14. camisole
15. slip

16. half slip
17. stockings
18. pantyhose
19. tights
20. socks
21. knee socks
22. shoes
23. (high) heels
24. pumps
25. loafers
26. sneakers

27. tennis shoes
28. running shoes
29. high tops/ high-top sneakers
30. sandals
31. thongs/flip-flops
32. boots
33. work boots
34. hiking boots
35. cowboy boots
36. moccasins

[1–21]
A. I can't find my new _____.
B. Did you look in the bureau/dresser/closet?
A. Yes, I did.
B. Then it's/they're probably in the wash.

[22–36]
A. Are those new _____?
B. Yes, they are.
A. They're very nice.
B. Thanks.

1. tee shirt
2. tank top
3. sweatshirt
4. sweat pants
5. running shorts
6. tennis shorts
7. lycra shorts
8. jogging suit/ running suit
9. leotard
10. tights
11. sweatband
12. coat
13. overcoat
14. jacket
15. windbreaker
16. ski jacket
17. bomber jacket
18. parka
19. down jacket
20. down vest
21. raincoat
22. poncho
23. trenchcoat
24. rubbers
25. gloves
26. mittens
27. hat
28. cap
29. baseball cap
30. beret
31. rain hat
32. ski hat
33. ski mask
34. ear muffs
35. scarf

[1–11]
A. Excuse me. I found this/these _____ in the dryer. Is it/Are they yours?
B. Yes. It's/They're mine. Thank you.

[12–35]
A. What's the weather like today?
B. It's cool/cold/raining/snowing.
A. I think I'll wear my _____.

Do you exercise? How? What kind of clothing and shoes do you wear when you exercise?

What do you wear outside when the weather is bad?

A. Oh, no! I think I lost my **ring**!
B. I'll help you look for it.

A. Oh, no! I think I lost my **earrings**!
B. I'll help you look for them.

1. ring
2. engagement ring
3. wedding ring/
wedding band
4. earrings
5. necklace
6. pearl necklace/
pearls

7. chain
8. beads
9. pin
10. watch/wrist watch
11. bracelet
12. cuff links

13. tie pin/tie tack
14. tie clip
15. belt
16. key ring/key chain
17. wallet
18. change purse
19. pocketbook/
purse/handbag

20. shoulder bag
21. tote bag
22. book bag
23. backpack
24. briefcase
25. umbrella

[In a store]
A. Excuse me. Is this/Are these
_____ on sale this week?
B. Yes. It's/They're half price.

[On the street]
A. Help! Police! Stop that
man/woman!
B. What happened?!
A. He/She just stole my _____
and my _____!

Do you like to wear jewelry? What
jewelry do you have?
In your country, what do men,
women, and children use to
carry their things?

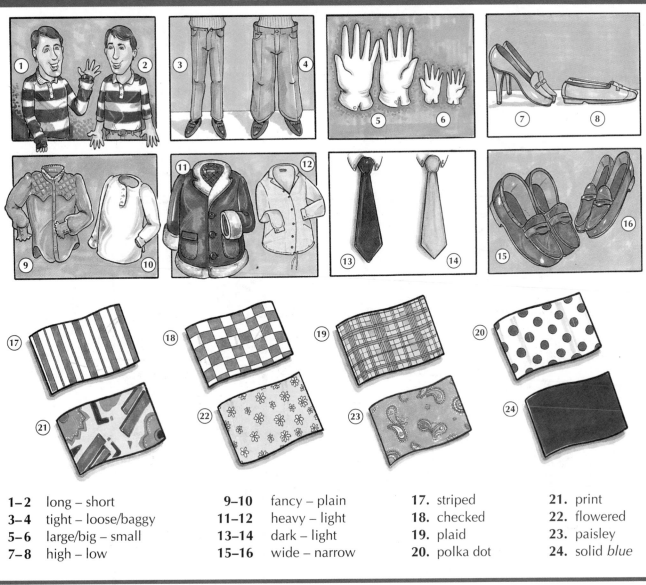

1–2	long – short	9–10	fancy – plain	17.	striped	21.	print
3–4	tight – loose/baggy	11–12	heavy – light	18.	checked	22.	flowered
5–6	large/big – small	13–14	dark – light	19.	plaid	23.	paisley
7–8	high – low	15–16	wide – narrow	20.	polka dot	24.	solid *blue*

[1–2]
A. Are the sleeves too **long**?
B. No. They're too **short**.

1–2	Are the sleeves too _____?	9–10	Is the blouse too _____?
3–4	Are the pants too _____?	11–12	Is the coat too _____?
5–6	Are the gloves too _____?	13–14	Is the color too _____?
7–8	Are the heels too _____?	15–16	Are the shoes too _____?

[17–24]
A. How do you like this _____ tie/shirt/skirt?
B. Actually, I prefer that _____ one.

Describe your favorite clothing.

A. Excuse me. Where's the **store directory**?
B. It's over there, next to the **escalator**.

1. (store) directory
2. escalator
3. Men's Clothing Department
4. Perfume Counter
5. Jewelry Counter
6. elevator
7. men's room
8. ladies' room

9. water fountain
10. parking garage
11. Women's Clothing Department
12. Children's Clothing Department
13. Housewares Department
14. Furniture Department/
    Home Furnishings Department
15. Household Appliances Department

16. Electronics Department
17. Customer Assistance Counter/
    Customer Service Counter
18. snack bar
19. Gift Wrap Counter
20. parking lot
21. customer pickup area

A. Pardon me. Is this the way to the
   _____?
B. Yes, it is./No, it isn't.

A. I'll meet you at/in/near/in front of
   the _____.
B. Okay. What time?
A. At *3:00*.

Describe a department store you
know. Tell what is on each floor.

A. May I help you?
B. Yes, please. I'm looking for a **TV**.

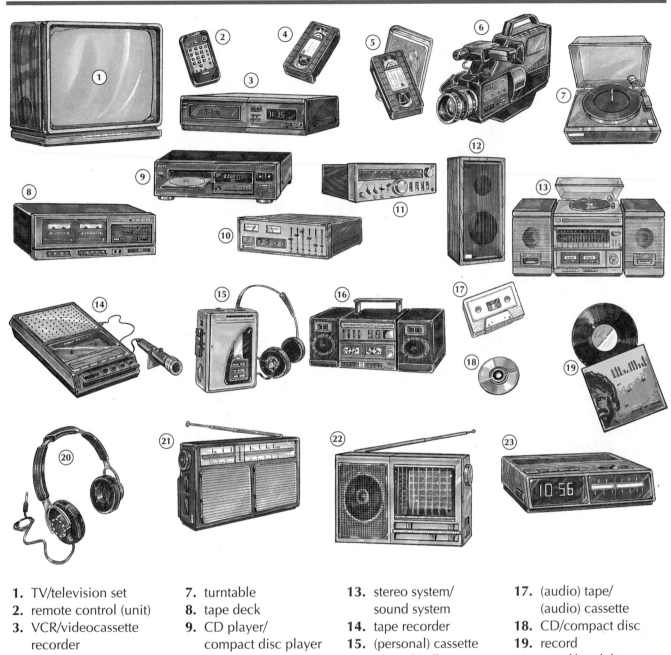

1. TV/television set
2. remote control (unit)
3. VCR/videocassette recorder
4. (blank) videotape
5. video/(video)tape
6. camcorder/ video camera
7. turntable
8. tape deck
9. CD player/ compact disc player
10. amplifier
11. tuner
12. speaker
13. stereo system/ sound system
14. tape recorder
15. (personal) cassette player/Walkman
16. portable stereo system/boom box
17. (audio) tape/ (audio) cassette
18. CD/compact disc
19. record
20. set of headphones
21. radio
22. shortwave radio
23. clock radio

A. How do you like my _____?
B. It's great/fantastic/awesome!

A. Which company makes a good _____?
B. In my opinion, the best _____ is made by ....

What video and audio equipment do you have or want?
In your opinion, which brands are the best?

A. Can you recommend a good **computer**?*
B. Yes. This **computer** here is excellent.

*With 9, use: Can you recommend good _____?

1. computer	8. (floppy) disk/diskette	15. fax machine	23. (movie) screen
2. monitor	9. (computer) software	16. camera	24. electric typewriter
3. disk drive	10. portable computer	17. zoom lens	25. electronic typewriter
4. keyboard	11. notebook computer	18. camera case	26. calculator
5. mouse	12. telephone/phone	19. flash attachment	27. adding machine
6. printer	13. portable phone/	20. tripod	28. voltage regulator
7. modem	portable telephone	21. film	29. adapter
	14. answering machine	22. slide projector	

A. Excuse me. Do you sell
_____s?†

B. Yes. We carry a complete line of
_____s.†

†With 9 and 21, use the singular.

A. Which _____ is the best?
B. This one here. It's made by
…………

Do you have a camera? What kind
is it? What do you take pictures of?
Does anyone you know have an
answering machine? When you
call, what does the machine say?
How have computers changed the
world?

A. Excuse me. I'm looking for (a/an) _____(s) for my *grandson*.*

B. Look in the next aisle.

A. Thank you.

* *grandson/granddaughter/...*

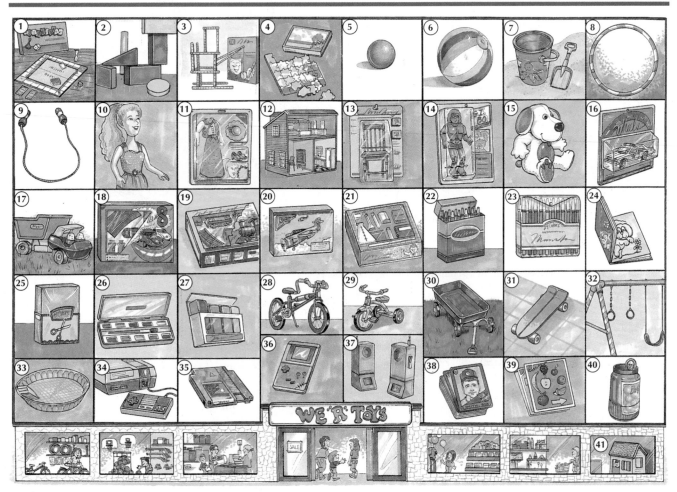

1. (board) game
2. (building) blocks
3. construction set
4. (jigsaw) puzzle
5. rubber ball
6. beach ball
7. pail and shovel
8. hula hoop
9. jump rope
10. doll
11. doll clothing
12. doll house
13. doll house furniture
14. action figure
15. stuffed animal
16. matchbox car
17. toy truck
18. racing car set
19. train set
20. model kit
21. science kit
22. crayons
23. (color) markers
24. coloring book
25. construction paper
26. paint set
27. (modeling) clay
28. bicycle
29. tricycle
30. wagon
31. skateboard
32. swing set
33. plastic swimming pool/ wading pool
34. video game system
35. (video) game cartridge
36. hand-held video game
37. walkie-talkie (set)
38. trading cards
39. stickers
40. bubble soap
41. play house

A. I don't know what to get my ....-year-old son/daughter for his/her birthday.
B. What about (a) _____?
A. Good idea! Thanks.

A. Mom/Dad? Can we buy this/these _____?
B. No, *Johnny*. Not today.

What toys are most popular in your country?
What were your favorite toys when you were a child?

Coins

Name	Value	Written as:
1. penny	one cent	1¢ $ .01
2. nickel	five cents	5¢ $ .05
3. dime	ten cents	10¢ $ .10
4. quarter	twenty-five cents	25¢ $ .25
5. half dollar	fifty cents	50¢ $ .50
6. silver dollar	one dollar	$1.00

A. How much is a **penny** worth?
B. A penny is worth **one cent**.

A. *Soda* costs *seventy-five cents.*
    Do you have enough change?
B. Yes. I have a/two/three _____(s) and . . . .

Currency

Name	We sometimes say:	Value	Written as:
7. (one-)dollar bill	a one	one dollar	$ 1.00
8. five-dollar bill	a five	five dollars	$ 5.00
9. ten-dollar bill	a ten	ten dollars	$ 10.00
10. twenty-dollar bill	a twenty	twenty dollars	$ 20.00
11. fifty-dollar bill	a fifty	fifty dollars	$ 50.00
12. (one-)hundred dollar bill	a hundred	one hundred dollars	$100.00

A. I need to go to the supermarket.
    Do you have any cash?
B. Let me see. I have a **twenty-dollar bill**.
A. **Twenty dollars** is enough. Thanks.

A. Can you change a **five-dollar bill/a five**?
B. Yes. I've got *five* **one-dollar bills**/*five ones*.

Written as	We say:	
$1.20	one dollar and twenty cents	How much do you pay for a loaf of bread? a hamburger?
	a dollar twenty	a cup of coffee? a gallon of gas?
$2.50	two dollars and fifty cents	Name and describe the coins and currency in your country.
	two fifty	What are they worth in U.S. dollars?
$37.43	thirty-seven dollars and forty-three cents	
	thirty-seven forty-three	

1. checkbook
2. check register
3. monthly statement
4. bank book
5. traveler's checks
6. credit card
7. ATM card

8. deposit slip
9. withdrawal slip
10. check
11. money order
12. loan application

13. (bank) vault
14. safe deposit box
15. teller
16. security guard
17. automatic teller (machine)/ ATM (machine)
18. bank officer

[1–7]
A. What are you looking for?
B. My _____. I can't find it/them anywhere!

[8–12]
A. What are you doing?
B. I'm filling out this _____.
A. For how much?
B. ....

[13–18]
A. How many _____s does the State Street Bank have?
B. ....

Do you have a bank account? What kind? Where?
Do you ever use traveler's checks? When?
Do you have a credit card? What kind? When do you use it?

[1–23, 27–79]

A. My doctor checked my **head** and said everything is okay.

B. I'm glad to hear that.

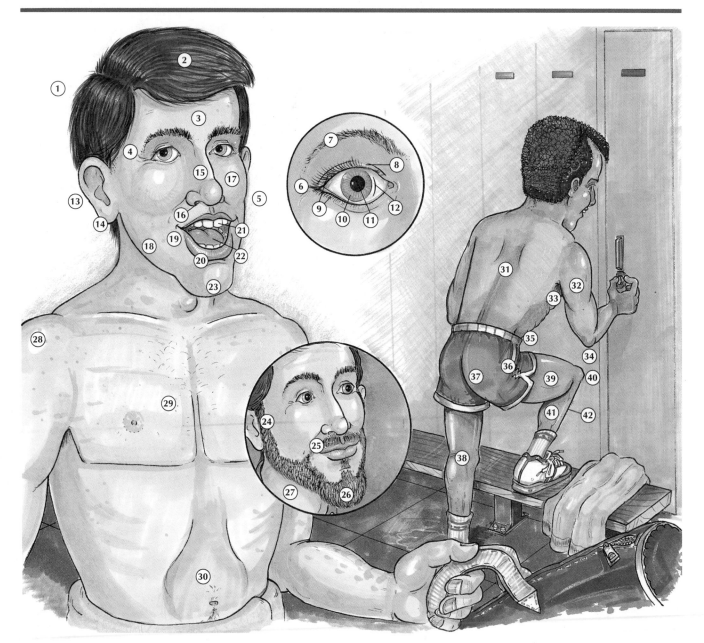

1. head	**11.** pupil	**21.** tooth–teeth	**31.** back	**37.** buttocks
2. hair	**12.** cornea	**22.** tongue	**32.** arm	**38.** leg
3. forehead	**13.** ear	**23.** chin	**33.** armpit	**39.** thigh
4. temple	**14.** earlobe	**24.** sideburn	**34.** elbow	**40.** knee
5. face	**15.** nose	**25.** mustache	**35.** waist	**41.** calf
6. eye	**16.** nostril	**26.** beard	**36.** hip	**42.** shin
7. eyebrow	**17.** cheek	**27.** neck		
8. eyelid	**18.** jaw	**28.** shoulder		
9. eyelashes	**19.** mouth	**29.** chest		
10. iris	**20.** lip	**30.** abdomen		

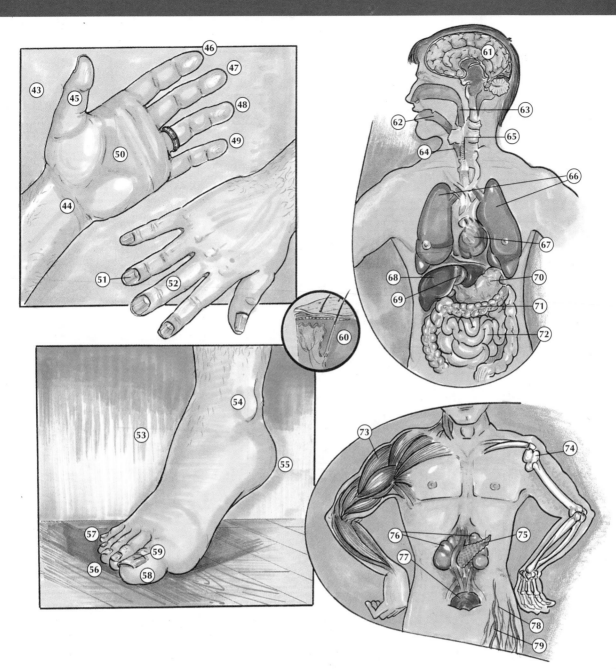

43. hand	**53.** foot	**61.** brain	**67.** heart	**73.** muscles
44. wrist	**54.** ankle	**62.** throat	**68.** liver	**74.** bones
45. thumb	**55.** heel	**63.** esophagus	**69.** gallbladder	**75.** pancreas
46. (index) finger	**56.** toe	**64.** windpipe	**70.** stomach	**76.** kidneys
47. middle finger	**57.** little toe	**65.** spinal cord	**71.** large intestine	**77.** bladder
48. ring finger	**58.** big toe	**66.** lungs	**72.** small intestine	**78.** veins
49. pinky/little finger	**59.** toenail			**79.** arteries
50. palm	**60.** skin			
51. fingernail				
52. knuckle				

[1, 3–8, 13–23, 27–34, 36–60]

A. Ooh!

B. What's the matter?

A. { My _____ hurts!
    { My _____ s hurt!

[61–79]

A. My doctor wants me to have some tests.

B. Why?

A. She's concerned about my _____.

Describe yourself as completely as you can.

Which parts of the body are most important at school? at work? when you play your favorite sport?

A. What's the matter?
B. I have a/an [1–19] .

A. What's the matter?
B. I have [20–26] .

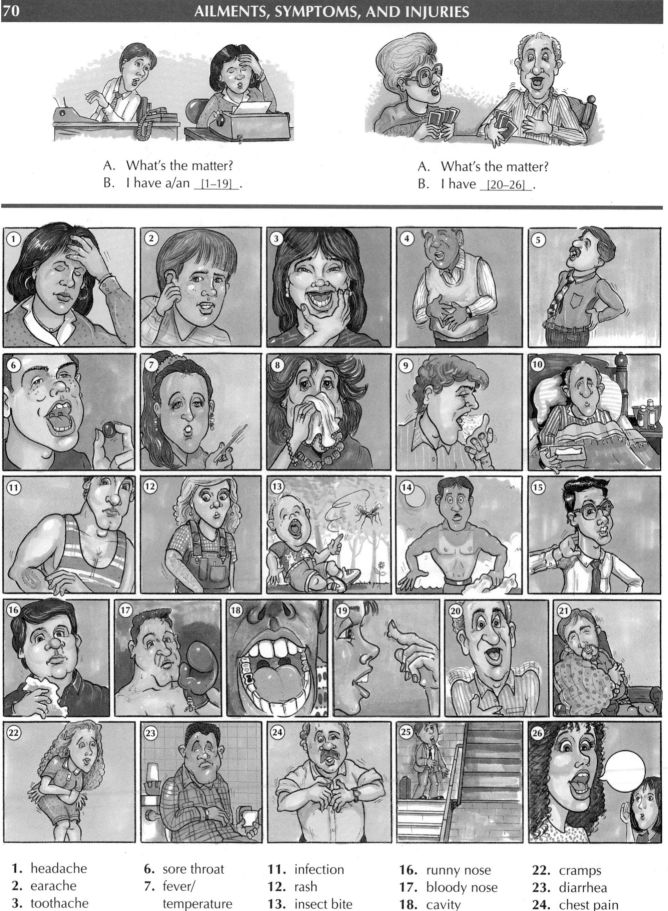

1. headache
2. earache
3. toothache
4. stomachache
5. backache

6. sore throat
7. fever/
   temperature
8. cold
9. cough
10. virus

11. infection
12. rash
13. insect bite
14. sunburn
15. stiff neck

16. runny nose
17. bloody nose
18. cavity
19. wart
20. (the) hiccups
21. (the) chills

22. cramps
23. diarrhea
24. chest pain
25. shortness of
   breath
26. laryngitis

A. What's the matter?
  B. { I feel __[27–30]__ .
      { I'm __[31–32]__ .
      { I'm __[33–38]__ ing.

A. What's the matter?
  B. { I __[39–48]__ ed my ....
      { My .... is/are __[49–50]__ .

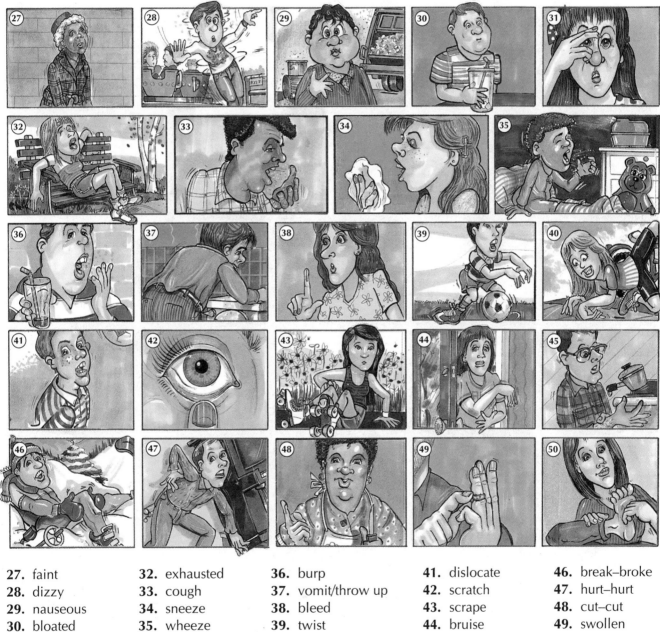

27. faint
28. dizzy
29. nauseous
30. bloated
31. congested

32. exhausted
33. cough
34. sneeze
35. wheeze

36. burp
37. vomit/throw up
38. bleed
39. twist
40. sprain

41. dislocate
42. scratch
43. scrape
44. bruise
45. burn

46. break–broke
47. hurt–hurt
48. cut–cut
49. swollen
50. itchy

A. How do you feel?
B. Not so good./Not very well./Terrible!
A. What's the matter?
B. ...., ..., and ....
A. I'm sorry to hear that.

Tell about the last time you didn't feel well. What was the matter?
Tell about a time you hurt yourself. What happened? How?
What are the symptoms of a cold? a heart problem?

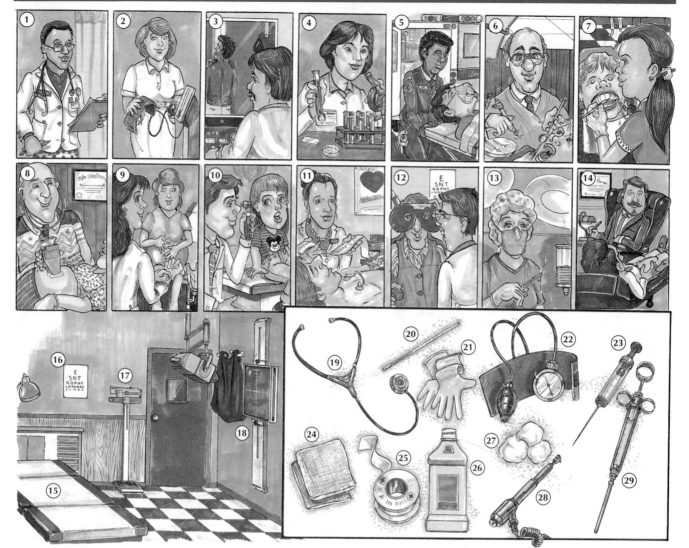

1. doctor/physician
2. nurse
3. X-ray technician
4. lab technician
5. EMT/emergency medical technician
6. dentist
7. (oral) hygienist

8. obstetrician
9. gynecologist
10. pediatrician
11. cardiologist
12. optometrist
13. surgeon
14. psychiatrist

15. examination table
16. eye chart
17. scale
18. X-ray machine
19. stethoscope
20. thermometer
21. gloves
22. blood pressure gauge

23. needle/syringe
24. bandages/gauze
25. adhesive tape
26. alcohol
27. cotton balls
28. drill
29. anesthetic/Novocaine

[1–14]
A. What do you do?
B. I'm a/an _____.

[15–18]
A. Please step over here to the _____.
B. Okay.

[19–29]
A. Please hand me the _____.
B. Here you are.

Where do you go for medical care? How often?
Who examines you? What does he/she do?

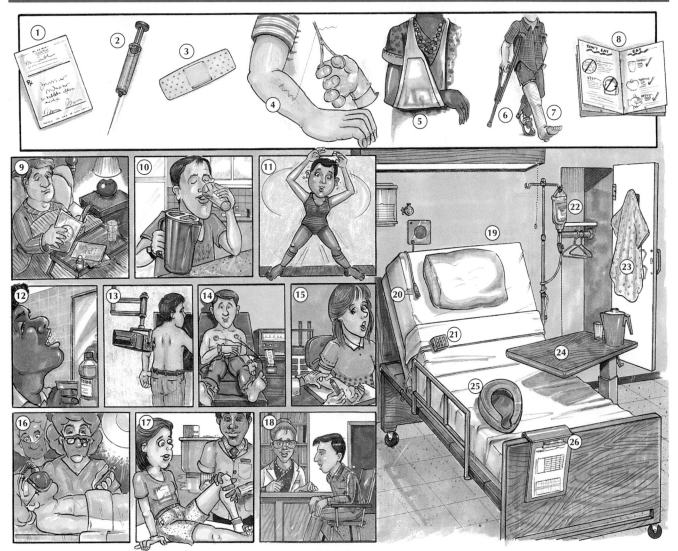

1. prescription
2. injection/shot
3. bandaid
4. stitches
5. sling
6. crutches
7. cast
8. diet

9. rest in bed
10. drink fluids
11. exercise
12. gargle
13. X-rays
14. tests
15. blood work/blood tests
16. surgery
17. physical therapy
18. counseling

19. hospital bed
20. call button
21. bed control
22. I.V.
23. hospital gown
24. bed table
25. bed pan
26. medical chart

[1–8]
A. What did the doctor do?
B. She/He gave me (a/an)
   _____.

[9–18]
A. What did the doctor say?
B. { She/He told me to [9–12] .
    { She/He told me I need [13–18] .

[19–26]
A. This is your _____.
B. I see.

When did you have your last medical checkup?
What did the doctor say?

Have you ever been in the hospital?
When? Why? Tell about your experience.

1. aspirin
2. cold tablets
3. vitamins
4. cough syrup
5. cough drops
6. throat lozenges
7. antacid tablets
8. decongestant spray/ nasal spray
9. eye drops
10. ointment
11. creme
12. lotion
13. heating pad
14. ice pack
15. wheelchair
16. pill
17. tablet
18. capsule
19. caplet
20. teaspoon
21. tablespoon

[1–15]
A. What did the doctor say?
B. { She/He told me to take [1–4].
   { She/He told me to use (a/an) [5–15].

[16–21]
A. What's the dosage?
B. One _____, every three hours.

What medicines do you take or use? For what ailments?

Describe any medical treatments or medicines in your country that are different from the ones in these lessons.

1. letter
2. postcard
3. air letter/ aerogramme
4. package/parcel
5. first class
6. air mail
7. parcel post
8. book rate/third class

9. registered mail
10. express mail/ overnight mail
11. stamp
12. sheet of stamps
13. roll of stamps
14. book of stamps
15. money order
16. change-of-address form

17. selective service registration form
18. envelope
19. address
20. zip code
21. return address
22. stamp/postage
23. postmark
24. mail slot
25. window

26. postal worker/ postal clerk
27. scale
28. stamp machine
29. mail truck
30. mailbox
31. letter carrier/ mail carrier
32. mail bag

[1–4]
A. Where are you going?
B. To the post office.
   I have to mail a/an _____.

[5–10]
A. How do you want to send it?
B. _____, please.

[11–17]
A. Next!
B. I'd like a _____, please.
A. Here you are.

[19–22]
A. Do you want me to mail this letter for you?
B. Yes, thanks.
A. Oops! You forgot the _____!

What time does your letter carrier deliver your mail? Does he/she drive a mail truck or carry a mail bag and walk?

Describe the post office you use:
   How many postal windows are there?
   Is there a stamp machine?
   Are the postal workers friendly?

Tell about the postal system in your country.

1. librarian	**9.** information desk	**16.** media section	**24.** journal
2. checkout desk	**10.** copier/	**17.** videotape	**25.** call card
3. library assistant	(photo)copy machine	**18.** record	**26.** call number
4. microfilm	**11.** reference librarian	**19.** tape	**27.** author
5. microfiche	**12.** reference section	**20.** computer diskette	**28.** title
6. card catalog	**13.** atlas	**21.** periodicals section	**29.** subject
7. online catalog	**14.** encyclopedia	**22.** newspaper	**30.** library card
8. shelves	**15.** dictionary	**23.** magazine	

[1–11]

A. Excuse me. Where's/
   Where are the _____?

B. Over there, at/near/next to
   the _____.

[12–24]

A. Excuse me. Where can I find
   a/an [13–15, 17–20, 22–24] ?

B. Look in the [12, 16, 21] over
   there.

[27–29]

A. May I help you?

B. Yes, please. I'm having
   trouble finding a book.

A. Do you know the _____?

B. Yes. …………

Do you go to a library? Which one? What does this library
have? Describe how you use the library.

1. office
2. nurse's office
3. guidance office
4. cafeteria
5. principal's office
6. classroom
7. locker

8. language lab
9. chemistry lab
10. teachers' lounge
11. gym/gymnasium
12. locker room
13. auditorium
14. field

15. bleachers
16. track
17. principal
18. assistant principal
19. (school) nurse
20. guidance counselor

21. lunchroom monitor
22. cafeteria worker
23. driver's ed instructor
24. teacher
25. coach
26. custodian

[1–16]
A. Where are you going?
B. I'm going to the _____.*
A. Do you have a hall pass?
B. Yes. Here it is.

*With 6 and 7, use: I'm going to my _____.

[17–26]
A. Who's that?
B. That's the new _____.

Describe the school where you study English. Tell about the rooms, offices, and people.

Tell about differences between schools in the United States and in your country.

1. math/mathematics
2. algebra
3. geometry
4. trigonometry
5. calculus

6. English
7. history
8. geography
9. science

10. biology
11. chemistry
12. physics
13. Spanish

14. French
15. home economics
16. health
17. industrial arts/shop

18. driver's education/
    driver's ed
19. typing
20. art
21. music

22. band
23. orchestra
24. choir/chorus

25. drama
26. football
27. school newspaper

28. yearbook
29. literary magazine
30. student government

[1–21]
A. What do you have next period?
B. _____. How about you?
A. _____.
B. There's the bell. I've got to go.

[22–30]
A. Are you going home right after school?
B. No. I have _[22–26]_ practice.
   No. I have a _[27–30]_ meeting.

What is/was your favorite subject? Why?
What extracurricular activities do/did you participate in?

A. What do you do?
B. I'm an **accountant**. How about you?
A. I'm a **carpenter**.

1. accountant	**4.** architect	**7.** baker	**10.** bricklayer/mason	**13.** carpenter
2. actor	**5.** artist	**8.** barber	**11.** bus driver	**14.** cashier
3. actress	**6.** assembler	**9.** bookkeeper	**12.** butcher	**15.** chef/cook

16. computer programmer
17. construction worker
18. courier/messenger
19. custodian/janitor
20. data processor
21. delivery person
22. electrician
23. farmer
24. firefighter
25. fisherman
26. foreman
27. gardener
28. hairdresser
29. housekeeper
30. journalist/reporter

[At a job interview]
A. Are you an experienced _____?
B. Yes. I'm a very experienced _____.

A. How long have you been a/an _____?
B. I've been a/an _____ for .... months/years.

Which of these occupations do you think are the most interesting? the most difficult? Why?

A. What's your occupation?
B. I'm a **lawyer**.
A. A **lawyer**?
B. Yes. That's right.

1. lawyer
2. mechanic
3. model

4. newscaster
5. painter
6. pharmacist

7. photographer
8. pilot
9. plumber

10. police officer
11. real estate agent
12. receptionist

13. repairperson
14. salesperson
15. sanitation worker

16. scientist

17. seamstress

18. secretary

19. security guard

20. stock clerk

21. tailor

22. taxi driver

23. teacher

24. translator/interpreter

25. travel agent

26. truck driver

27. waiter

28. waitress

29. welder

30. veterinarian

A. Are you still a _____?
B. No. I'm a _____.
A. Oh. That's interesting.

A. What kind of job would you like in the future?
B. I'd like to be a _____.

Do you work? What's your occupation?
What are the occupations of people in your family?

A. Can you **act**?
B. Yes, I can.

1. act
2. assemble *components*
3. bake
4. build *things*/construct *things*
5. clean

6. cook
7. deliver *pizzas*
8. design *buildings*
9. draw
10. drive *a truck*

11. file
12. fly *an airplane*
13. grow *vegetables*
14. guard *buildings*

15. mow *lawns*
16. operate *equipment*
17. paint
18. play the *piano*
19. repair *things*/fix *things*

20. sell *cars*
21. serve *food*
22. sew
23. sing
24. teach

25. translate
26. type
27. wash *dishes*
28. write

A. What do you do for a living?
B. I _____.

A. Do you know how to _____?
B. Yes. I've been _____ing for years.

Tell about your work abilities.
What can you do?

1. reception area
2. coat rack
3. coat closet
4. message board
5. mailbox
6. file cabinet
7. supply cabinet
8. storage cabinet
9. workstation

10. computer workstation
11. water cooler
12. coffee cart
13. office
14. mailroom
15. postage machine/ postage meter
16. copier/ (photo)copy machine

17. waste receptacle
18. supply room
19. storage room
20. conference room
21. conference table
22. whiteboard/ dry erase board
23. employee lounge
24. coffee machine
25. soda machine

26. receptionist
27. typist
28. file clerk
29. secretary
30. administrative assistant
31. office manager
32. office assistant
33. employer/boss

[1–25]
A. Where's ....?
B. { He's/She's in the/his/her _____.*
    { He's/She's at the/his/her _____.†

*1, 13, 14, 18–20, 23   †2–12, 15–17, 21, 22, 24, 25

[26–33]
A. Who's he/she?
B. He's/She's the new _____.

Describe an office you are familiar with.
Tell about the rooms, the work areas, and the employees.

A. Do you know how to work this **computer**?
B. No, I don't.
A. Let me show you how.

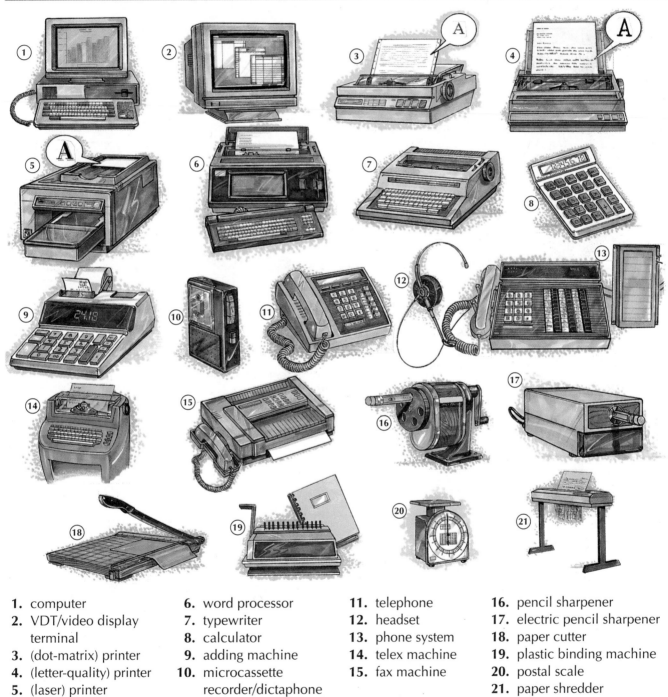

1. computer
2. VDT/video display terminal
3. (dot-matrix) printer
4. (letter-quality) printer
5. (laser) printer

6. word processor
7. typewriter
8. calculator
9. adding machine
10. microcassette recorder/dictaphone

11. telephone
12. headset
13. phone system
14. telex machine
15. fax machine

16. pencil sharpener
17. electric pencil sharpener
18. paper cutter
19. plastic binding machine
20. postal scale
21. paper shredder

A. I think this _____ is broken!
B. I'll take a look at it.

A. Have you seen the new _____?
B. No, I haven't.
A. It's much better than the old one!

Do you know how to operate a computer? a fax machine? Give step-by-step instructions for using some type of office equipment.

1. desk
2. swivel chair
3. rolodex
4. pencil cup
5. letter tray/
   stacking tray
6. memo holder
7. desk calendar
8. desk lamp
9. nameplate

10. desk pad
11. wastebasket
12. posture chair/
    clerical chair
13. wall calendar
14. wall planner
15. file cabinet
16. stapler
17. staple remover
18. tape dispenser

19. paper clip dispenser
20. business cards
21. clipboard
22. appointment book
23. organizer/
    personal planner
24. timesheet
25. paycheck
26. letter opener
27. scissors

28. punch
29. 3-hole punch
30. stamp pad/ink pad
31. rubber stamp
32. pen
33. pencil
34. mechanical pencil
35. highlighter (pen)
36. eraser

[1–15]
A. Welcome to the company.
B. Thank you.
A. How do you like your _____?
B. It's/They're very nice.

[16–36]
A. My desk is such a mess! I can't find
   my _____!
B. Here it is/Here they are next to your
   _____.

Which items on this page do you have? Do you have an appointment
book, personal planner, or calendar? How do you remember
important things such as appointments, meetings, and birthdays?

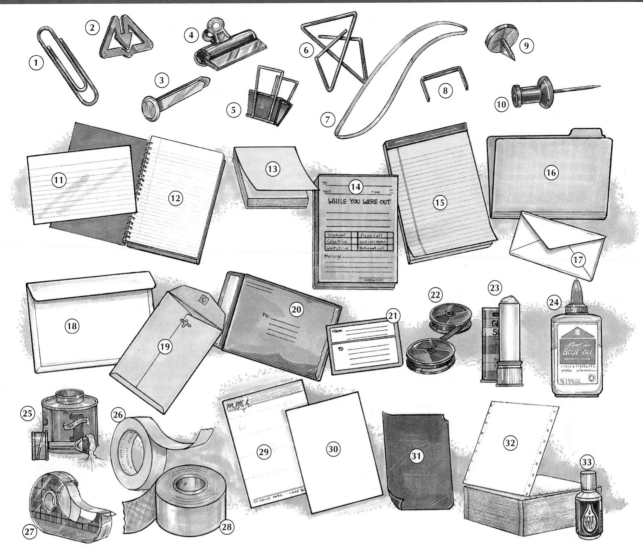

1. paper clip
2. plastic clip
3. paper fastener
4. bulldog clip
5. binder clip
6. clamp
7. rubber band
8. staple
9. thumbtack

10. pushpin
11. index card
12. memo pad/note pad
13. Post-It note pad
14. message pad
15. legal pad
16. file folder/
    manila folder
17. envelope

18. catalog envelope
19. clasp envelope
20. mailer
21. mailing label
22. typewriter ribbon
23. gluestick
24. glue
25. rubber cement
26. masking tape

27. Scotch tape/
    cellophane tape
28. sealing tape/
    package mailing tape
29. stationery
30. typing paper
31. carbon paper
32. computer paper
33. correction fluid

A. We've run out of __[1–23]__ s.
    We've run out of __[24–33]__ .
B. I'll get some more from the supply room.

A. Could I borrow a/an/some __[1–33]__ ?
B. Sure. Here you are.

Which supplies do you use? What do you use them for?
Where do you buy them?

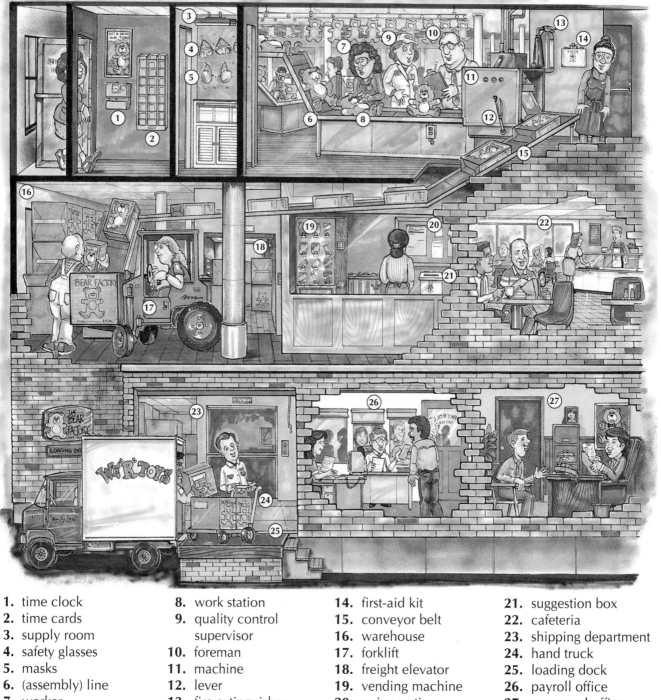

1. time clock
2. time cards
3. supply room
4. safety glasses
5. masks
6. (assembly) line
7. worker

8. work station
9. quality control supervisor
10. foreman
11. machine
12. lever
13. fire extinguisher

14. first-aid kit
15. conveyor belt
16. warehouse
17. forklift
18. freight elevator
19. vending machine
20. union notice

21. suggestion box
22. cafeteria
23. shipping department
24. hand truck
25. loading dock
26. payroll office
27. personnel office

A. Excuse me. I'm a new employee.
    Where's/Where are the _____?
B. Next to/Near/In/On the _____.

A. Have you seen *Fred*?
B. Yes. He's in/on/at/next to/near
    the _____.

Are there any factories where you live? What kind?
What are the working conditions there?

What products do factories in your country produce?

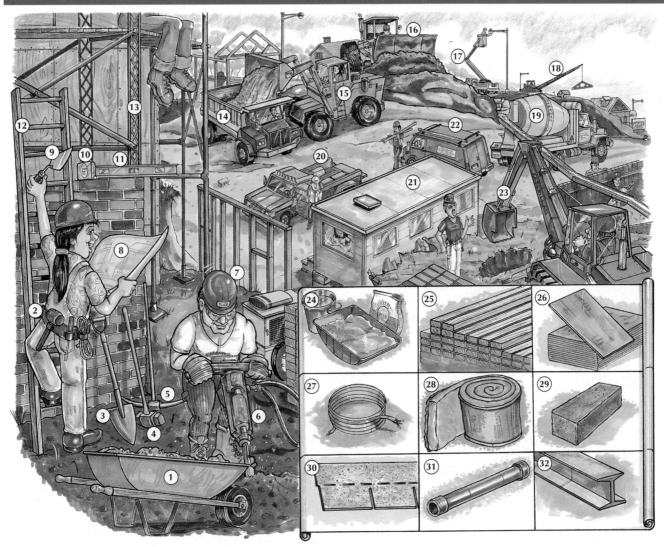

1. wheelbarrow
2. toolbelt
3. shovel
4. sledgehammer
5. pickax
6. jackhammer/ pneumatic drill
7. helmet/hard hat
8. blueprints
9. trowel
10. tape measure
11. level
12. ladder
13. scaffolding
14. dump truck
15. front-end loader
16. bulldozer
17. cherry picker
18. crane
19. cement mixer
20. pickup truck
21. trailer
22. van
23. backhoe
24. cement
25. wood/lumber
26. plywood
27. wire
28. insulation
29. brick
30. shingle
31. pipe
32. girder/beam

[1–12]
A. Could you get me that/those _____?
B. Sure.

[13–23]
A. Watch out for that _____!
B. Oh! Thanks for the warning!

[24–32]
A. Are we going to have enough [24–28] / [29–32] s to finish the job?
B. I think so.

What building materials is your home made of? When was it built?

Tell about a construction site near your home or school. Describe what you see.

1. headlight
2. bumper
3. turn signal
4. parking light
5. tire
6. hubcap
7. hood
8. windshield
9. windshield wipers
10. side mirror
11. antenna
12. sunroof
13. luggage rack/
    luggage carrier
14. rear windshield
15. rear defroster
16. trunk
17. taillight
18. brake light
19. backup light
20. license plate
21. tailpipe
22. muffler
23. transmission
24. gas tank
25. jack
26. spare tire
27. flare
28. jumper cables
29. engine
30. spark plugs
31. carburetor
32. air filter
33. battery
34. dipstick
35. alternator
36. radiator
37. fan belt
38. radiator hose
39. gas station/
    service station
40. air pump
41. service bay
42. mechanic
43. attendant
44. gas pump
45. nozzle

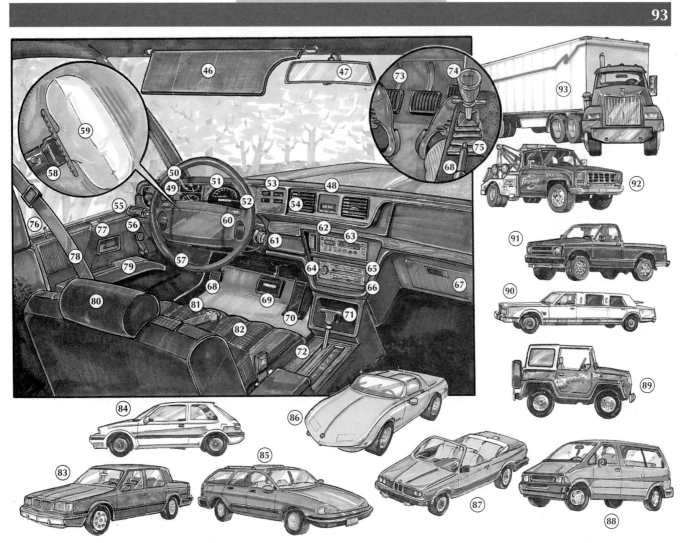

46. visor	**57.** steering wheel	**70.** accelerator/gas pedal	**83.** sedan
47. rearview mirror	**58.** steering column	**71.** gearshift	**84.** hatchback
48. dashboard/	**59.** air bag	**72.** automatic transmission	**85.** station wagon
instrument panel	**60.** horn	**73.** clutch	**86.** sports car
49. gas gauge/fuel gauge	**61.** ignition	**74.** stickshift	**87.** convertible
50. temperature gauge	**62.** radio	**75.** manual transmission	**88.** minivan
51. speedometer	**63.** tape deck/cassette player	**76.** door lock	**89.** jeep
52. odometer	**64.** air conditioning	**77.** door handle	**90.** limousine
53. warning lights	**65.** heater	**78.** shoulder harness	**91.** pick-up truck
54. vent	**66.** defroster	**79.** armrest	**92.** tow truck
55. turn signal	**67.** glove compartment	**80.** headrest	**93.** truck
56. cruise control	**68.** emergency brake	**81.** seat belt	
	69. brake	**82.** seat	

[1, 3, 8–15, 23, 34–38, 46–82]

A. What's the matter with your car?
B. The _____(s) is/are broken.

[1, 4–6, 9–11, 30–33, 37, 38]

A. Can I help you?
B. Yes. I need to replace a/the _____(s).

[1, 2, 4–8, 10–14, 16–20]

A. I was just in a car accident!
B. Oh, no! Were you hurt?
A. No. But my _____(s) was/were damaged.

Do you own a car? What kind? Which of the features on pages 92–93 does your car have? Tell about any repairs your car has needed.

1. tunnel
2. bridge
3. tollbooth
4. exact change lane
5. route sign
6. highway
7. road
8. divider/barrier
9. overpass
10. underpass

11. entrance ramp/ on ramp
12. interstate (highway)
13. median
14. left lane
15. middle lane/ center lane
16. right lane
17. shoulder
18. broken line
19. solid line

20. speed limit sign
21. exit (ramp)
22. exit sign
23. yield sign
24. service area
25. railroad crossing
26. street
27. one-way street
28. double yellow line
29. crosswalk

30. intersection
31. school crossing
32. corner
33. traffic light/ traffic signal
34. no left turn sign
35. no right turn sign
36. no U-turn sign
37. do not enter sign
38. stop sign

A. Where's the accident?
B. It's on/in/at/near the _____.

Describe a highway you travel on.
Describe an intersection near where you live.

In your area, on which highways and streets do most accidents occur? Why are these places dangerous?

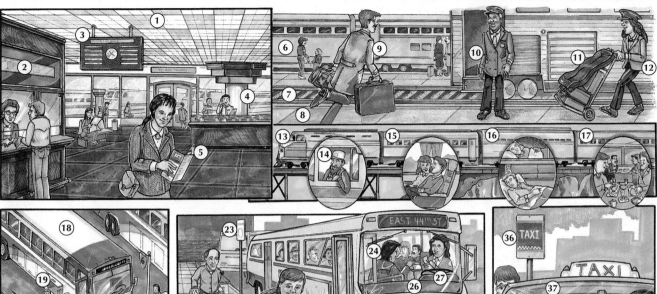

A. train
1. train station
2. ticket window
3. arrival and departure board
4. information booth
5. schedule/timetable
6. train
7. track
8. platform
9. passenger
10. conductor

11. luggage/baggage
12. porter/redcap
13. engine
14. engineer
15. passenger car
16. sleeper
17. dining car

B. bus
18. bus
19. luggage compartment/ baggage compartment
20. bus driver

21. bus station
22. ticket counter

C. local bus
23. bus stop
24. rider/passenger
25. (bus) fare
26. fare box
27. transfer

D. subway
28. subway station
29. subway

30. token booth
31. turnstile
32. commuter
33. (subway) token
34. fare card
35. fare card machine

E. taxi
36. taxi stand
37. taxi/cab/taxicab
38. meter
39. fare
40. cab driver/taxi driver

[A–E]
A. How are you going to get there?
B. { I'm going to take the _[A–D]_ .
{ I'm going to take a _[E]_ .

[1–8, 10–23, 26, 28–31, 35, 36]
A. Excuse me. Where's the _____?
B. Over there.

How do you get to school or work?
Describe public transportation where you live.

In your country, can you travel far by train or by bus? Where can you go? How much do tickets cost? Describe the buses and trains.

A. Check-In
1. ticket counter
2. ticket agent
3. ticket
4. arrival and departure monitor

B. Security
5. security checkpoint
6. security guard
7. X-ray machine
8. metal detector

C. The Gate
9. check-in counter
10. boarding pass
11. gate
12. waiting area
13. concession stand/ snack bar
14. gift shop
15. duty-free shop

D. Baggage Claim
16. baggage claim (area)
17. baggage carousel
18. suitcase
19. luggage carrier
20. garment bag
21. baggage
22. porter/skycap
23. (baggage) claim check

E. Customs and Immigration
24. customs
25. customs officer
26. customs declaration form
27. immigration
28. immigration officer
29. passport
30. visa

[1, 2, 4–9, 11–17, 24, 25, 27, 28]
A. Excuse me. Where's the _____?*
B. Right over there.

*With 24 and 27, use: Excuse me. Where's _____?

[3, 10, 18–21, 23, 26, 29, 30]
A. Oh, no! I think I've lost my _____!
B. I'll help you look for it.

Describe an airport you are familiar with. Tell about the check-in area, security, concession stands, and the baggage claim area.

Have you ever gone through Customs and Immigration? Tell about your experience.

1. cockpit
2. pilot/captain
3. co-pilot
4. instrument panel
5. flight engineer
6. first-class section
7. passenger
8. galley
9. flight attendant
10. lavatory/bathroom
11. cabin
12. carry-on bag
13. overhead compartment
14. aisle
15. seat belt
16. window seat
17. middle seat
18. aisle seat
19. Fasten Seat Belt sign
20. No Smoking sign
21. call button
22. oxygen mask
23. emergency exit
24. armrest
25. seat control
26. tray (table)
27. meal
28. seat pocket
29. emergency instruction card
30. air sickness bag
31. life vest
32. runway
33. terminal (building)
34. control tower
35. airplane/plane/jet
36. nose
37. fuselage
38. cargo door
39. landing gear
40. wing
41. engine
42. tail
43. propeller plane/prop
44. propeller
45. helicopter
46. rotor (blade)

A. Where's the _____?
B. In/On/Next to/Behind/In front of/Above/ Below the _____.

Ladies and gentlemen. This is your captain speaking. I'm sorry for the delay. We had a little problem with one of our _____s.* Everything is fine now and we'll be taking off shortly.

*Use 4, 7, 10, 12, 20–22, 24.

Have you ever flown in an airplane? Tell about a flight you have taken. Describe the plane, your seat, and the meal.

Be a flight attendant! Give your passengers instructions before takeoff.

A. Weather

1. sunny
2. cloudy
3. clear
4. hazy
5. foggy
6. windy
7. humid/muggy
8. raining
9. drizzling
10. snowing
11. hailing
12. sleeting
13. lightning
14. thunderstorm
15. snowstorm
16. hurricane/ typhoon
17. tornado

B. Temperature

18. thermometer
19. Fahrenheit
20. Centigrade/Celsius
21. hot
22. warm
23. cool
24. cold
25. freezing

C. Seasons

26. summer
27. fall/autumn
28. winter
29. spring

[1–12]
A. What's the weather like?
B. It's _____.

[13–17]
A. What's the weather forecast?
B. There's going to be
   _[13]_ /a _[14–17]_ .

[19–25]
A. How's the weather?
B. It's _[21–25]_ .
A. What's the temperature?
B. It's ……. degrees _[19, 20]_ .

Describe the seasons where you live.
Tell about the weather and the temperature.

What's your favorite season?
Why?

A. camping
1. tent
2. backpack
3. sleeping bag
4. tent stakes
5. hatchet

6. lantern
7. camp stove

B. hiking
8. hiking boots
9. compass
10. trail map

C. mountain climbing
11. hiking boots

D. rock climbing
12. rope
13. harness

E. picnic
14. (picnic) blanket
15. thermos
16. picnic basket

[A–E]
A. Let's go _____* this weekend.
B. Good idea! We haven't gone _____*
in a long time.

*With E, say: on a picnic

[1–16]
A. Did you bring the _____?
B. Yes, I did.

Have you ever gone camping or hiking?
Where? What equipment did you use?

Do you like to go on picnics? Where?
What picnic supplies and food do you take with you?

1. jogging path
2. rest rooms
3. statue
4. picnic area
5. picnic table
6. grill

7. trash can
8. merry-go-round/ carousel
9. fountain
10. zoo
11. water fountain

12. band shell
13. bridle path
14. bike rack
15. duck pond
16. bicycle path/ bikeway

17. bench
18. playground
19. jungle gym
20. monkey bars
21. slide
22. swings

23. tire swing
24. seesaw
25. wading pool
26. sandbox
27. sand

[1–18]
A. Excuse me. Does this park have (a) _____?
B. Yes. Right over there.

[19–27]
A. { Be careful on the [19–24] !
{ Be careful in the [25–27] !
B. I will, Mom/Dad.

Describe a park and a playground you are familiar with.

1. lifeguard
2. lifeguard stand
3. life preserver
4. snack bar/refreshment stand
5. sand dune
6. rock
7. swimmer
8. wave
9. surfer
10. vendor
11. sunbather
12. sand castle
13. seashell/shell
14. beach umbrella
15. (beach) chair
16. (beach) towel
17. bathing suit/swimsuit
18. bathing cap
19. kickboard
20. surfboard
21. kite
22. raft/air mattress
23. tube
24. (beach) blanket
25. sun hat
26. sunglasses
27. suntan lotion/sunscreen
28. pail/bucket
29. shovel
30. beach ball
31. cooler

[1–13]
A. What a nice beach!
B. It is. Look at all the _____s!

[14–31]
A. Are you ready for the beach?
B. Almost. I just have to get my _____.

Do you like to go to the beach? Describe your favorite beach. What do you take when you go there?

A. jogging
1. jogging suit
2. jogging shoes

B. running
3. running shorts
4. running shoes

C. walking
5. walking shoes

D. roller skating
6. roller skates
7. knee pads

E. cycling/bicycling/biking
8. bicycle/bike
9. (bicycle) helmet

F. skateboarding
10. skateboard
11. elbow pads

G. bowling
12. bowling ball
13. bowling shoes

H. horseback riding
14. saddle
15. reins
16. stirrups

I. skydiving
17. parachute

J. golf
18. golf clubs
19. golf ball

K. tennis
20. tennis racquet
21. tennis ball

L. squash
22. squash racquet
23. squash ball

M. handball
24. handball glove
25. handball

N. racquetball
26. safety goggles
27. racquetball
28. racquet

O. ping pong
29. paddle
30. ping pong table
31. net
32. ping pong ball

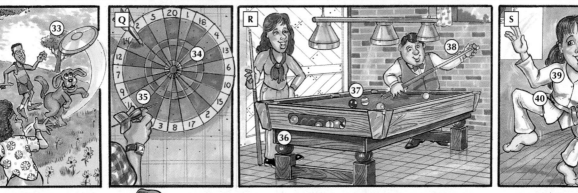

P. frisbee
33. frisbee

Q. darts
34. dartboard
35. darts

R. billiards/pool
36. pool table
37. billiard balls
38. pool stick

S. karate
39. karate outfit
40. karate belt

T. gymnastics
41. balance beam
42. parallel bars
43. mat
44. horse
45. trampoline

U. weightlifting
46. barbell
47. weights

V. archery
48. bow and arrow
49. target

W. box
50. boxing gloves
51. (boxing) trunks

X. wrestle
52. wrestling uniform
53. (wrestling) mat

Y. work out
54. universal/
    exercise equipment
55. exercise bike

[A–Y]
A. What do you like to do in your free time?
B. {
  I like to go [A–I] .
  I like to play [J–R] .
  I like to do [S–V] .
  I like to [W–Y] .
}

[1–55]
A. I really like this/these new _____.
B. It's/They're very nice.

Do you do any of these activities? Which ones?
Which are popular in your country?

[A–H]
A. Do you like **baseball**?
B. Yes. **Baseball** is one of my favorite sports.

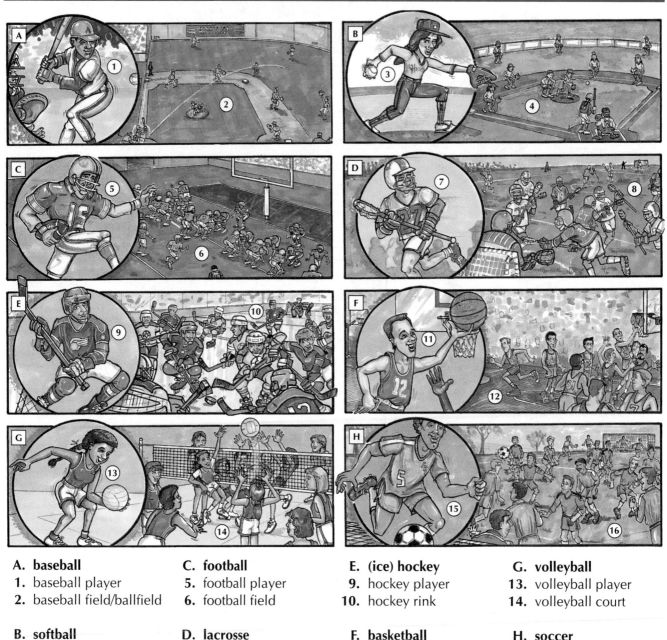

A. **baseball**	C. **football**	E. **(ice) hockey**	G. **volleyball**
1. baseball player	5. football player	9. hockey player	13. volleyball player
2. baseball field/ballfield	6. football field	10. hockey rink	14. volleyball court

B. **softball**	D. **lacrosse**	F. **basketball**	H. **soccer**
3. softball player	7. lacrosse player	11. basketball player	15. soccer player
4. ballfield	8. lacrosse field	12. basketball court	16. soccer field

A. .... plays [A–H] very well.
B. You're right. I think he's/she's one
    of the best _____s* on the team.

Use 1, 3, 5, 7, 9, 11, 13, 15.

A. Now, listen! I want all of you
    to go out on that _____† and
    play the best game of [A–H]
    you've ever played!
B. All right, Coach!

†*Use 2, 4, 6, 8, 10, 12, 14, 16.*

Which sports on this page do you like
    to play? Which do you like to
    watch?
What are your favorite teams?
Name some famous players of these
    sports.

[1–27]
A. I can't find my **baseball**!
B. Look in the *closet.**

*closet, basement, garage

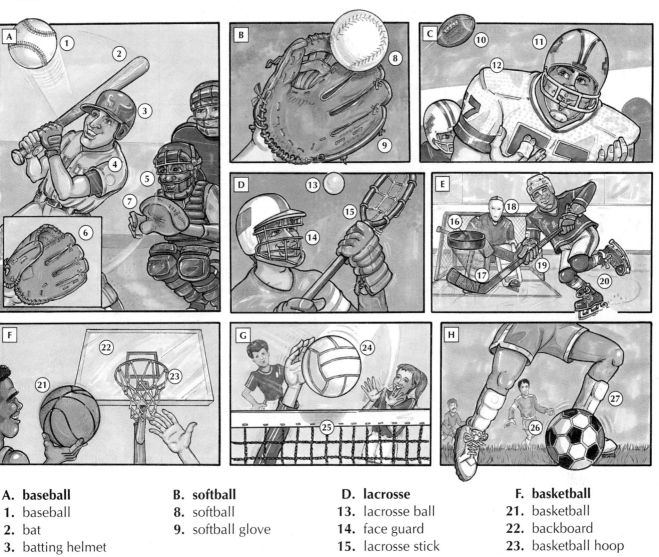

A. baseball	**B. softball**	**D. lacrosse**	**F. basketball**
1. baseball	8. softball	13. lacrosse ball	21. basketball
2. bat	9. softball glove	14. face guard	22. backboard
3. batting helmet		15. lacrosse stick	23. basketball hoop
4. baseball uniform	**C. football**		
5. catcher's mask	10. football	**E. hockey**	**G. volleyball**
6. baseball glove	11. football helmet	16. hockey puck	24. volleyball
7. catcher's mitt	12. shoulder pads	17. hockey stick	25. volleyball net
		18. hockey mask	
		19. hockey glove	**H. soccer**
		20. hockey skates	26. soccer ball
			27. shinguards

[In a store]
A. Excuse me. I'm looking for (a) [1–27] .
B. All our [A–H] equipment is over there.
A. Thanks.

[At home]
A. I'm going to play [A–H] after school today.
B. Don't forget your [1–21, 24–27] !

Which sports on this page are popular in your country? Which sports are played in high school?

[A–H]
A. What's your favorite winter sport?
B. **Skiing**.

A. (downhill) skiing
1. skis
2. ski boots
3. bindings
4. poles

B. cross-country skiing
5. cross-country skis

C. (ice) skating
6. (ice) skates
7. skate guards

D. figure skating
8. figure skates

E. sledding
9. sled
10. sledding dish/saucer

F. bobsledding
11. bobsled

G. snowmobiling
12. snowmobile

H. tobogganing
13. toboggan

[A–H]
[At work or at school on Friday]
A. What are you going to do this weekend?
B. I'm going to go _____.

[1–13]
[On the telephone]
A. Hello. Jimmy's Sporting Goods.
B. Hello. Do you sell _____(s)?
A. Yes, we do./No, we don't.

Have you ever watched the Winter Olympics? What is your favorite event? Which event do you think is the most exciting? the most dangerous?

[A–L]
A. Would you like to go **sailing** tomorrow?
B. Sure. I'd love to.

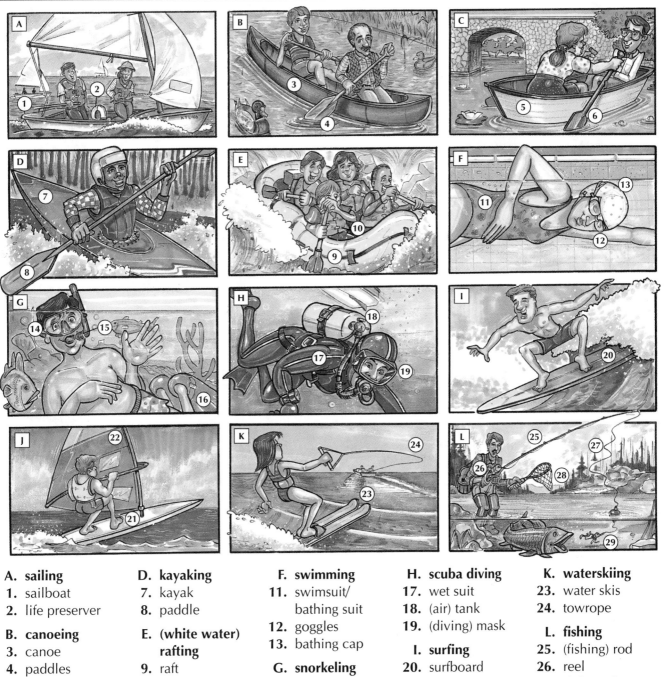

A. sailing
1. sailboat
2. life preserver

B. canoeing
3. canoe
4. paddles

C. rowing
5. rowboat
6. oars

D. kayaking
7. kayak
8. paddle

E. (white water) rafting
9. raft
10. life jacket

F. swimming
11. swimsuit/ bathing suit
12. goggles
13. bathing cap

G. snorkeling
14. mask
15. snorkel
16. flippers

H. scuba diving
17. wet suit
18. (air) tank
19. (diving) mask

I. surfing
20. surfboard

J. windsurfing
21. sailboard
22. sail

K. waterskiing
23. water skis
24. towrope

L. fishing
25. (fishing) rod
26. reel
27. (fishing) line
28. net
29. bait

A. Have you ever gone [A–L] ?
B. Yes, I have./No, I haven't.

A. Do you have everything you need to go [A–L] ?
B. Yes. I have my [1–29] (and my [1–29]).
A. Have a good time.

Which sports on this page have you tried? Which sports would you like to try?
Are any of these sports popular in your country? Which ones?

1. hit	**8.** bounce	**15.** hop	**22.** swing	**29.** push-up
2. pitch	**9.** dribble	**16.** skip	**23.** push	**30.** sit-up
3. throw	**10.** shoot	**17.** jump	**24.** pull	**31.** leg lift
4. catch	**11.** stretch	**18.** kneel	**25.** lift	**32.** jumping jack
5. pass	**12.** bend	**19.** sit	**26.** swim	**33.** deep knee bend
6. kick	**13.** walk	**20.** lie down	**27.** dive	**34.** somersault
7. serve	**14.** run	**21.** reach	**28.** shoot	**35.** cartwheel
				36. handstand

[1–10]
A. _____ the ball!
B. Okay, Coach!

[11–28]
A. Now _____!
B. Like this?
A. Yes.

[29–36]
A. Okay, everybody. I want
    you to do twenty _____s!
B. Twenty _____s?!
A. That's right.

Do you exercise regularly?
Which exercises do you do?

Be an exercise instructor. Lead your friends in an exercise
routine using the actions on this page.

[A–Q]
A. What's your hobby?
B. **Sewing.**

A. sewing
1. sewing machine
2. pin
3. pin cushion
4. thread
5. (sewing) needle
6. thimble
7. material

B. knitting
8. knitting needle
9. yarn

C. weaving
10. loom

D. crocheting
11. crochet hook

E. needlepoint

F. embroidery

G. quilting

H. painting
12. paintbrush
13. easel
14. paint

I. sculpting/sculpture
15. plaster
16. stone

J. pottery
17. clay
18. potter's wheel

K. woodworking

L. stamp collecting
19. stamp album

M. coin collecting
20. coin catalog
21. coin album

N. model building
22. model kit
23. (model) glue
24. (model) paint

O. bird watching
25. binoculars
26. field guide

P. photography
27. camera

Q. astronomy
28. telescope

R. games
29. chess
30. checkers
31. backgammon
32. Monopoly
33. Scrabble
34. cards
35. Trivial Pursuit
36. marbles
37. jacks

[1–28]
     [In a store]
A. May I help you?
B. Yes, please. I'd like to buy
  (a/an) _____.

[29–37]
     [At home]
A. What do you want to do?
B. Let's play _____.

What's your hobby?
What games are popular in your
  country? Describe how to play one.

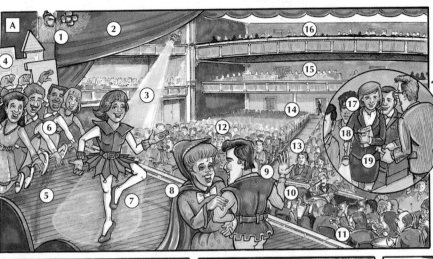

A. theater
1. lights/lighting
2. curtain
3. spotlight
4. scenery
5. stage
6. chorus
7. dancer
8. actress
9. actor

10. orchestra
11. orchestra pit
12. audience
13. aisle
14. orchestra
15. mezzanine
16. balcony
17. usher
18. program
19. ticket

B. symphony
20. symphony orchestra
21. musician
22. conductor
23. baton
24. podium

C. opera
25. opera singer
26. opera company

D. ballet
27. ballet dancer

28. ballerina
29. ballet company
30. ballet slippers
31. toeshoes

E. movies
32. marquee
33. box office
34. billboard
35. lobby
36. refreshment stand
37. (movie) screen

[A–E]
A. What are you doing this evening?
B. I'm going to the _____.

[1–11, 20–37]
A. { What a magnificent _____!
   { What magnificent _____s!
B. I agree.

[14–16]
A. Where did you sit during the performance?
B. We sat in the _____.

What kinds of entertainment on this page are popular in your country?

Tell about a play, concert, opera, ballet, or movie you have seen. Describe the performance and the theater.

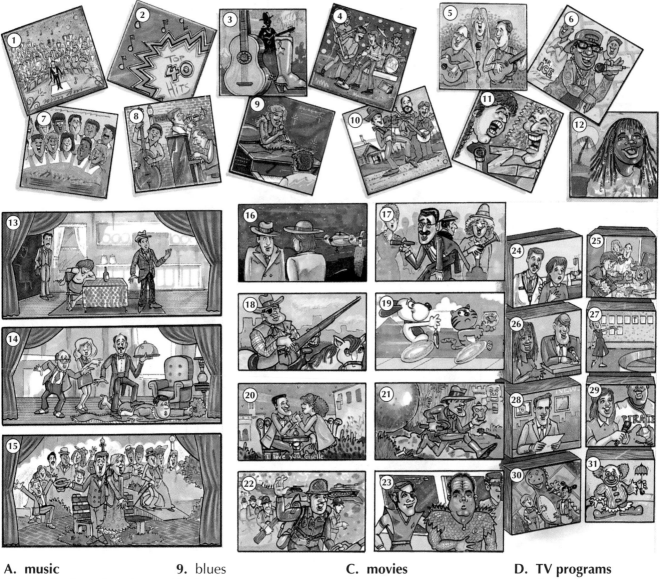

A. music
1. classical music
2. popular music
3. country music
4. rock music
5. folk music
6. rap music
7. gospel music
8. jazz

9. blues
10. bluegrass
11. heavy metal
12. reggae

B. plays
13. drama
14. comedy
15. musical (comedy)

C. movies
16. drama
17. comedy
18. western
19. cartoon
20. foreign film
21. adventure movie
22. war movie
23. science fiction movie

D. TV programs
24. drama
25. (situation) comedy/ sitcom
26. talk show
27. game show
28. news program
29. sports program
30. children's program
31. cartoon

A. What kind of _[A–D]_ do you like?
B. { I like _[1–12]_ .
{ I like _[13–31]_ s.

What's your favorite type of music?
Who is your favorite singer? musician? musical group?

What kind of movies do you like?
Who are your favorite movie stars?
What are the titles of your favorite movies?

What kind of TV programs do you like?
What are your favorite shows?

A. Do you play a musical instrument?
B. Yes. I play the **violin**.

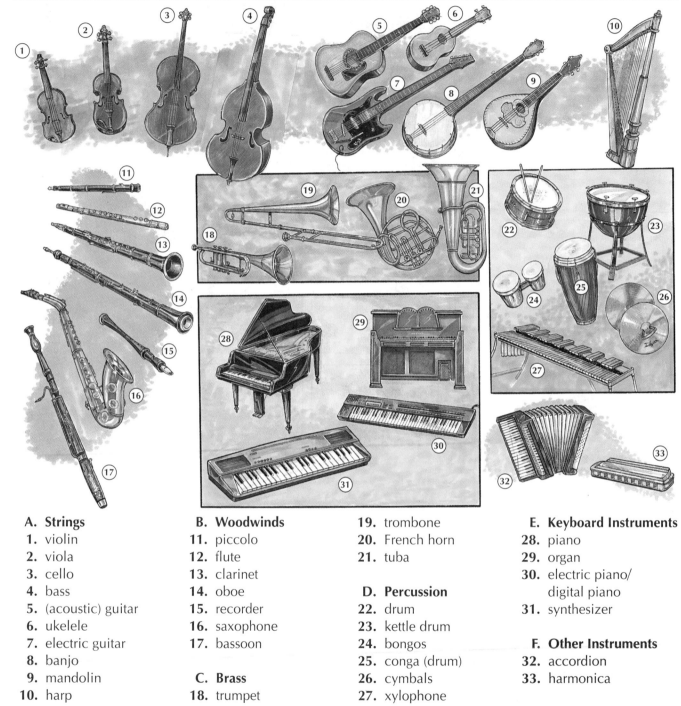

A. Strings
1. violin
2. viola
3. cello
4. bass
5. (acoustic) guitar
6. ukelele
7. electric guitar
8. banjo
9. mandolin
10. harp

B. Woodwinds
11. piccolo
12. flute
13. clarinet
14. oboe
15. recorder
16. saxophone
17. bassoon

C. Brass
18. trumpet

19. trombone
20. French horn
21. tuba

D. Percussion
22. drum
23. kettle drum
24. bongos
25. conga (drum)
26. cymbals
27. xylophone

E. Keyboard Instruments
28. piano
29. organ
30. electric piano/
   digital piano
31. synthesizer

F. Other Instruments
32. accordion
33. harmonica

A. You play the _____ very well.
B. Thank you.

A. What's that noise?
B. That's my son/daughter
   practicing the _____.

Do you play a musical instrument?
   Which one?
Which instruments are usually in an
   orchestra? a marching band?
   a rock music group?
Name and describe other musical
   instruments used in your country.

1. tree
2. leaf–leaves
3. twig
4. branch
5. limb
6. trunk
7. bark
8. root
9. needle
10. cone

11. dogwood
12. holly
13. magnolia
14. elm
15. cherry
16. palm
17. birch
18. maple
19. oak
20. pine

21. redwood
22. (weeping) willow
23. flower
24. petal
25. pistula
26. stamen
27. stem
28. bud
29. thorn
30. bulb

31. chrysanthemum/
    mum
32. daffodil
33. daisy
34. gardenia
35. lily
36. pansy
37. petunia
38. orchid
39. rose
40. sunflower

41. tulip
42. violet
43. bush
44. shrub
45. fern
46. plant
47. cactus–cacti
48. vine
49. grass
50. poison ivy

[11–22]
A. What kind of tree is that?
B. I think it's a/an _____ tree.

[31–48]
A. Look at all the _____s!
B. They're beautiful!

Describe your favorite tree and your favorite flower.
What kinds of trees and flowers grow where you live?

In your country, are flowers used at weddings? at funerals?
on holidays? on visits to the hospital? Tell which flowers are
used for different occasions.

1. forest/woods	8. hill	15. river	22. ocean	29. oil
2. lake	9. field	16. dam	23. island	30. (natural) gas
3. meadow	10. stream/brook	17. desert	24. air pollution	31. coal
4. mountain	11. pond	18. dune	25. acid rain	32. wind
5. valley	12. plateau	19. jungle	26. toxic waste	33. nuclear energy
6. waterfall	13. cliff	20. seashore	27. radiation	34. solar energy
7. rapids	14. canyon	21. bay	28. water pollution	35. hydroelectric power

[1–23]
A. { Isn't this a beautiful _____?!
     { Aren't these beautiful _____?!
B. It's/They're magnificent.

[24–28]
A. Do you worry about the environment?
B. Yes. I'm very concerned about _____.

Describe some places of natural beauty in your country.

What kind of energy do you use to heat your home? to cook?
In your opinion, which kind of energy is best for producing electricity?

1. farmhouse	**8.** stable	**16.** orchard	**24.** rooster	**32.** bull
2. (vegetable) garden	**9.** hay	**17.** fruit tree	**25.** chicken/hen	**33.** (dairy) cow
3. scarecrow	**10.** pitchfork	**18.** farmer	**26.** chick	**34.** calf–calves
4. crop	**11.** barnyard	**19.** hired hand	**27.** turkey	**35.** horse
5. irrigation system	**12.** pig pen/pig sty	**20.** chicken coop	**28.** goat	**36.** pig
6. barn	**13.** field	**21.** hen house	**29.** kid	**37.** piglet
7. silo	**14.** combine	**22.** fence	**30.** sheep	
	15. pasture	**23.** tractor	**31.** lamb	

A. Where's the _____?
B. In/On/Next to the _____.

A. The [24–37] s got loose again!
B. Oh, no! Where are they?
A. They're in the [1, 2, 12, 13, 15, 16, 20, 21] !

Tell about farms in your country.
What crops and animals are common on these farms?

1. fox	**8.** mouse–mice	**18.** donkey	**27.** leopard	**31.** tiger
2. porcupine	**9.** chipmunk	**19.** buffalo	**a.** spots	**a.** paw
a. quill	**10.** rat	**20.** camel	**28.** giraffe	**32.** lion
3. raccoon	**11.** squirrel	**a.** hump	**29.** bison	**a.** mane
4. wolf–wolves	**12.** rabbit	**21.** llama	**30.** elephant	**33.** hippopotamus
5. moose	**13.** gopher	**22.** horse	**a.** tusk	**34.** hyena
a. antler	**14.** beaver	**a.** tail	**b.** trunk	**35.** rhinoceros
6. deer	**15.** bat	**23.** foal		**a.** horn
a. hoof	**16.** skunk	**24.** pony		**36.** zebra
7. fawn	**17.** possum	**25.** armadillo		**a.** stripes
		26. kangaroo		
		a. pouch		

37. black bear	**41.** panda	**46.** orangutan	**Pets**		**54.** puppy
a. claw	**42.** monkey	**47.** gorilla	**51.** cat		**55.** hamster
38. grizzly bear	**43.** chimpanzee	**48.** anteater	**a.** whiskers		**56.** gerbil
39. polar bear	**44.** gibbon	**49.** worm	**52.** kitten		**57.** guinea pig
40. koala (bear)	**45.** baboon	**50.** slug	**53.** dog		

[1–50]
A. Look at that _____!
B. Wow! That's the biggest _____
I've ever seen!

[51–57]
A. Do you have a pet?
B. Yes. I have a _____.
A. What's your _____'s name?
B. …………

What animals can be found where you live?
Is there a zoo near where you live? What animals does the zoo have?
What are some common pets in your country?

If you were an animal, which animal do you think you would be? Why?
Does your culture have any popular folk tales or children's stories about animals? Tell a story you are familiar with.

A. Birds

1. robin
  a. nest
  b. egg
2. blue jay
  a. wing
  b. tail
  c. feather
3. cardinal
4. hummingbird
5. pheasant
6. crow
7. seagull

8. sparrow
9. woodpecker
  a. beak
10. swallow
11. pigeon
12. owl
13. hawk
14. eagle
  a. claw
15. canary
16. cockatoo
17. parrot
18. parakeet

19. duck
  a. bill
20. duckling
21. goose
22. swan
23. flamingo
24. crane
25. stork
26. pelican
27. peacock
28. penguin
29. roadrunner
30. ostrich

B. Insects

31. fly
32. mosquito
33. flea
34. firefly/
  lightning bug
35. moth
36. dragonfly
37. spider
  a. web
38. ladybug
39. wasp
40. tick

41. bee
  a. beehive
42. caterpillar
  a. cocoon
43. butterfly
44. grasshopper
45. ant
46. beetle
47. termite
48. roach/cockroach
49. scorpion
50. centipede
51. praying mantis
52. cricket

[1–52]

A. Is that a/an _____?

B. No. I think it's a/an _____.

[31–52]

A. Hold still! There's a _____ on your shirt!

B. Oh! Can you get it off of me?

A. There! It's gone!

What birds and insects can be found where you live?

Does your culture have any popular folk tales or children's stories about birds or insects? Tell a story you are familiar with.

A. Fish

1. trout
   a. fin
   b. gill
   c. tail
2. bass
3. salmon
4. shark
5. flounder
6. swordfish
7. eel
8. sea horse

B. Sea Animals

9. whale
10. dolphin
11. seal
    a. flipper
12. jellyfish
13. otter
14. walrus
    a. tusk
15. lobster
    a. claw
16. crab
17. octopus
    a. tentacle
18. shrimp
19. mussel
20. clam
21. scallop
22. oyster
23. snail
24. starfish
25. squid

C. Amphibians and Reptiles

26. tortoise
    a. shell
27. turtle
28. alligator
29. crocodile
30. lizard
31. iguana
32. tadpole
33. frog
34. salamander
35. snake
36. rattlesnake
37. cobra
38. boa constrictor

[1–38]
A. Is that a/an _____?
B. No. I think it's a/an _____.

[26–38]
A. Are there any _____s around here?
B. No. But there are lots of _____s.

What fish, sea animals, and reptiles can be found in your country? Which ones are endangered and need to be protected? Why?

In your opinion, which ones are the most interesting? the most beautiful? the most dangerous?

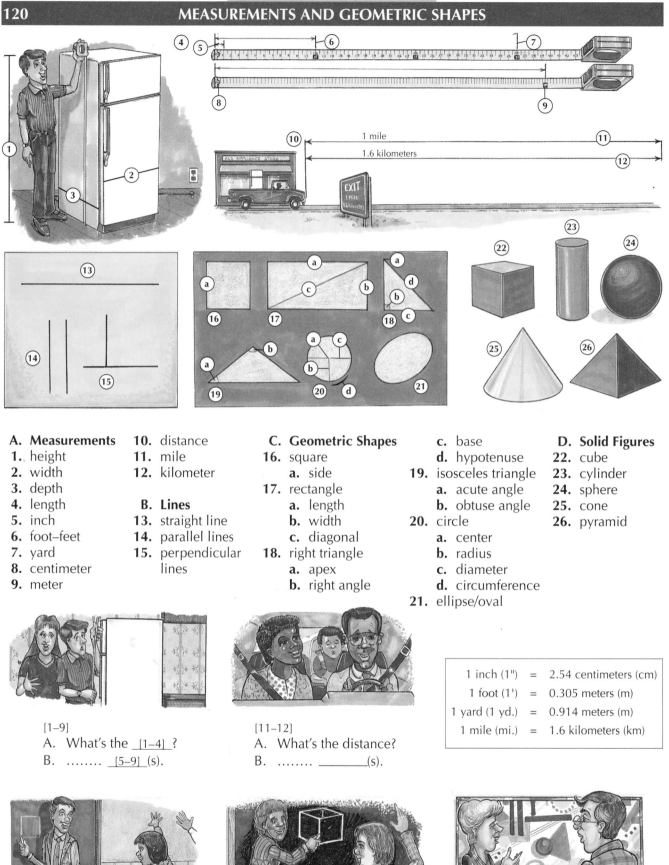

A. Measurements
1. height
2. width
3. depth
4. length
5. inch
6. foot–feet
7. yard
8. centimeter
9. meter

10. distance
11. mile
12. kilometer

B. Lines
13. straight line
14. parallel lines
15. perpendicular
    lines

C. Geometric Shapes
16. square
    a. side
17. rectangle
    a. length
    b. width
    c. diagonal
18. right triangle
    a. apex
    b. right angle

    c. base
    d. hypotenuse
19. isosceles triangle
    a. acute angle
    b. obtuse angle
20. circle
    a. center
    b. radius
    c. diameter
    d. circumference
21. ellipse/oval

D. Solid Figures
22. cube
23. cylinder
24. sphere
25. cone
26. pyramid

[1–9]
A. What's the [1–4] ?
B. .... [5–9] (s).

[11–12]
A. What's the distance?
B. .... _____(s).

1 inch (1")	=	2.54 centimeters (cm)
1 foot (1')	=	0.305 meters (m)
1 yard (1 yd.)	=	0.914 meters (m)
1 mile (mi.)	=	1.6 kilometers (km)

[16–21]
A. Who can tell me what
    shape this is?
B. I can. It's a/an _____.

[22–26]
A. Who knows what figure
    this is?
B. I do. It's a/an _____.

[13–26]
A. This painting is magnificent!
B. Hmm. I don't think so. It just
    looks like a lot of _____s
    and _____s to me!

A. The Universe
1. galaxy
2. star
3. constellation
   a. The Big Dipper
   b. The Little Dipper

B. The Solar System
4. sun
5. moon
6. planet
7. solar eclipse
8. lunar eclipse
9. meteor
10. comet
11. asteroid
12. Mercury
13. Venus
14. Earth
15. Mars
16. Jupiter
17. Saturn
18. Uranus
19. Neptune
20. Pluto

C. Space Exploration
21. satellite
22. (space) probe
23. space craft/orbiter
24. space station
25. astronaut
26. space suit
27. rocket
28. launch pad
29. space shuttle
30. booster rocket
31. mission control
32. U.F.O./Unidentified Flying Object/ flying saucer

[1–20]
A. Is that (a/an/the) _____?
B. I'm not sure. I think it might be (a/an/the) _____.

[21–27, 29, 31]
A. Is the _____ ready for tomorrow's launch?
B. Yes. "All systems are go!"

Pretend you are an astronaut traveling in space. What do you see?
Draw and name a constellation you are familiar with.

Do you think space exploration is important? Why?
Have you ever seen a U.F.O.? Do you believe there is life in outer space? Why?

The bold number indicates the page(s) on which the word appears; the number that follows indicates the word's location in the illustration and in the word list on the page. For example, "north **5**-1" indicates that the word *north* is on page 5 and is item number 1.

Cardinal Numbers 30

1	one
2	two
3	three
4	four
5	five
6	six
7	seven
8	eight
9	nine
10	ten
11	eleven
12	twelve
13	thirteen
14	fourteen
15	fifteen
16	sixteen
17	seventeen
18	eighteen
19	nineteen
20	twenty
21	twenty-one
22	twenty-two
30	thirty
40	forty
50	fifty
60	sixty
70	seventy
80	eighty
90	ninety
100	one hundred
101	one hundred (and) one
102	one hundred (and) two
1,000	one thousand
10,000	ten thousand
100,000	one hundred thousand
1,000,000	one million

Ordinal Numbers 30

1st	first
2nd	second
3rd	third
4th	fourth
5th	fifth
6th	sixth
7th	seventh
8th	eighth
9th	ninth
10th	tenth
11th	eleventh
12th	twelfth
13th	thirteenth
14th	fourteenth
15th	fifteenth
16th	sixteenth
17th	seventeenth
18th	eighteenth
19th	nineteenth
20th	twentieth
21st	twenty-first
22nd	twenty-second
30th	thirtieth
40th	fortieth
50th	fiftieth
60th	sixtieth
70th	seventieth
80th	eightieth
90th	ninetieth
100th	one hundredth
101st	one hundred (and) first
102nd	one hundred (and) second
1,000th	one thousandth
10,000th	ten thousandth
100,000th	one hundred thousandth
1,000,000th	one millionth

Days of the Week 33

Sunday
Monday
Tuesday
Wednesday
Thursday
Friday
Saturday

Months of the Year 33

January
February
March
April
May
June
July
August
September
October
November
December